# DEVOTIONS®

**SEPTEMBER**

> They never stopped teaching and proclaiming the
> good news that Jesus is the Messiah.
>
> —*Acts 5:42*

**Gary Wilde,** Editor    **Margaret Williams,** Project Editor    Photo Brand X Pictures | Thinkstock®

*DEVOTIONS*® is published quarterly by Standard Publishing, Cincinnati, Ohio, www.standardpub.com.
© 2014 by Standard Publishing. All rights reserved. Topics based on the Home Daily Bible Readings,
International Sunday School Lessons. © 2012 by the Committee on the Uniform Series. Printed in
the U.S.A. All Scripture quotations, unless otherwise indicated, are taken from the *HOLY BIBLE,
NEW INTERNATIONAL VERSION*®. *NIV*®. Copyright © 1973, 1978, 1984, 2011 by Biblica, Inc.®
Used by permission of Zondervan. All rights reserved worldwide. *New American Standard Bible*®,
(*NASB*) Copyright © 1960, 1962, 1963, 1968, 1971, 1972, 1973, 1975, 1977, 1995 by The Lock-
man Foundation. Used by permission. (www.Lockman.org). *Holy Bible, New Living Translation*
(*NLT*), © 1996, 2004, 2007. Tyndale House Publishers. Scripture quotations marked (*NKJV*) are
taken from the *New King James Version*®. Copyright © 1982 by Thomas Nelson, Inc. Used by
permission. All rights reserved.                                    Volume 58 No. 4

# Norm's Legacy

**You are not the one to build the temple, but your son, your own flesh and blood—he is the one** (2 Chronicles 6:9).

**Scripture:** 2 Chronicles 6:1-15
**Song:** "Now Thank We All Our God"

We need to remind ourselves, and others, that our life on earth is short. Our "big picture" life plan, all we set out to accomplish, is likely to be interrupted by death. But God reminds us that our legacy lives on in our loved ones.

Our daughters and their spouses, our beautiful grandchildren, all were washed, combed, and shiny in their church clothes. Bursting with pride, they lined up right in the front pews, glowing, standing in the sunbeams filtered through stained glass. They assembled to share seemingly small—but hugely important—ways in which life is forever better because of their dad, their dad-in-law, and their Grandpa Norm.

Next, there were Norm's "prodigies"—youngsters who had worked for and learned from Norm over the years. Five of these, now successful young men, had followed in Norm's footsteps in choosing their own careers. Each stood up to share his memories and gratitude, even telling how Norm had been like a father to them. And they have been, really, like sons to us.

My friend Marietta said it perfectly, "There stands Norm's legacy, right here in front of us. He must be so very proud."

Thank You, **precious Lord,** for loving us. Thank You for the part we get to play in God's big picture. Teach us how to play and be grateful. In Your name, amen.

September 1–6. **Anne Collins** lives in Venice, Florida. Her interests are faith, family, friends, food, flowers, fitness, and fabrics.

# Jennifer's Song

Sorrowful, yet always rejoicing; poor, yet making many rich; having nothing, and yet possessing everything (2 Corinthians 6:10).

**Scripture:** 2 Corinthians 6:1-13
**Song:** "Take My Hand, Precious Lord"

Jennifer showed unusual maturity, confidence, creativity, and outstanding leadership qualities. She was one of my former students, a 9-year-old fourth grader. Her big, struggling, non-church-going family would probably have been labeled "dysfunctional." Her parents divorced when Jen was 10, and her mom began moving all over the country with the kids, facing one derailment after another.

Oh, by the way—God chose Jennifer to be one of His co-workers! Jen became a Christian, and this spring she graduated from the University of North Carolina. Now she's working toward her master's degree in theology.

She writes to me: "I just got a new job working for a study-abroad program out of the university called the Atlantis Project. The program allows students to gain work experience in medical or education fields in the Azores, a group of islands off the coast of Portugal. I will be organizing student internships and events. And I could not be more excited! This is quite an unexpected but blessed opportunity. God has done amazing things in my life since graduation, and I feel so blessed to follow Him."

**Dearest Father,** I fill up with joy and gratitude when I witness Your loving hand leading a precious child into Your service. Thank You for allowing me to share the very beginning of Jen's amazing story. In Jesus' name, amen.

# Anne's Song

**I will do whatever you ask in my name, so that the Father may be glorified in the Son** (John 14:13).

**Scripture:** John 14:11-13
**Song:** "Thank You, Lord"

The boy I married 53 years ago was becoming a stranger, fading into a world of physical disability and dementia. And I wasn't ready to accept the situation. Praying for strength and understanding, I was led to accept Jesus' total presence in my life and to accept my own vital role as Norm's caregiver. Gradually I learned to accept the facts too: *Norm's illness is terminal. It will get worse. It won't be pretty.*

Yet Jesus taught me to accept help. Resources presented themselves: kind doctors and caring neighbors, our daughters and their families, our church and local fire and rescue personnel. All, in a sense, came to my rescue. Then there were the physical therapists, the hospice volunteers, and the people who would call—or just show up—exactly when their help was needed.

Specialists installed safety equipment in our home. The Senior Friendship Center offered caregiver support classes. I was blessed to meet people facing situations similar to ours. It became clear that we could give Norm the loving care he needed. One day at a time, we did just that.

Eventually, Norm passed away, peacefully, in our living room, surrounded by his family. We accept, and we are grateful for, God's peace. As I look ahead, I will do whatever He asks.

**Heavenly Father,** I am blessed just now with an overwhelming love for Norm, for my precious family, and for Jesus my Lord. In His name, amen.

# Mary's Song

**It is by the name of Jesus Christ of Nazareth, whom you crucified but whom God raised from the dead, that this man stands before you healed** (Acts 4:10).

**Scripture:** Acts 4:1-12
**Song:** "O Bless the Lord, My Soul"

My dear friend Mary is a talented, beloved, first-grade teacher in Michigan. Mary started a prayer group for our school staff, and we'd meet briefly every Wednesday morning before the school day began. We'd pray with and for each other, and about whatever school issues might be bubbling up. We'd praise God, then go about our week feeling blessed, refreshed, and confident.

One day Mary couldn't figure out how to drive home. *Glitch.* The next day, she couldn't read the clock. *Ooops.* Her doctor found a dangerous brain tumor, with surgery required.

But Mary wasn't afraid. She'd given her life to Christ years ago and looked forward to going to Heaven some day. So off she went to the hospital. The rest of us weren't taking it lightly. We prayed: for Mary, for the doctors, for a miracle. We couldn't live without her. *Don't call her home now. Please, God.* Weeks of uncertainty followed.

Then Mary breezed back to school, glowing, more beautiful than ever, a pretty scarf tied around her head. She's been in remission for 12 years.

Teaching is both an art and a craft. Mary is an artist and a craftswoman. She does it for Jesus.

Thank You, **Lord,** for life. Teach me, and all of us, to discover our spiritual gifts and to do our crafts for Jesus and His kingdom. In His name, amen.

# Diana's Song

**As for us, we cannot help speaking about what we have seen and heard** (Acts 4:20).

**Scripture:** Acts 4:13-22
**Song:** "Come, Holy Spirit, Heavenly Dove"

My friend Diana calls it "living in expectation." When she and I make eye contact, we quietly open our palms to the heavens and spontaneously break into smiles of recognition and joy. It's sort of like a secret between friends. But it's not a secret. We have developed the habit of looking forward to witnessing miracles that happen every day.

It requires awareness, though—awareness of, and acceptance of, each blessing. Then I find myself saying "Thank You, God," or "Thank You, Jesus," many times each day.

Continually expressing gratitude has increased my awareness of the work of the Holy Spirit. This morning I phoned my new friend, Judy, to invite her to my quilting circle meeting. "Oh, my, yes!" she exclaimed. "I'm so happy. I can't wait to show you my quilts." (I'd had no idea Judy was interested in quilting.) And over coffee that afternoon, my friend Rosario delighted me with wonderful stories of her childhood in Mexico.

Working in my kitchen, I recently found my engagement ring that I had lost—52 years ago! And tonight, on the anniversary of first receiving my ring, our daughter invited me to dinner. I would have been alone—how did she know?

Thank You, **God,** for the miracles You offer to our view every day. When I look, let me truly see Your hand at work, in me, in the friends around me, and in the world at large. May I live in expectation this day. In Jesus' name. Amen.

# Norm's Song

**"Sovereign Lord," they said, "you made the heavens and the earth and the sea, and everything in them"** (Acts 4:24).

**Scripture:** Acts 4:23-31
**Song:** This Is My Father's World

My husband told delightful stories of his childhood in western New York. His family lived in a sparsely populated, wonderfully scenic, rural region near Lake Erie. There Norm and his brother explored nearby farms, hills and valleys, lakes and forests, wetlands, rock formations, and waterfalls. Norm and Donnie were brave little explorers, even experts, immensely knowledgeable about local plants and wildlife habitats.

Recently I was delighted to discover that the hymn "This Is My Father's World," was penned by a man who lived in the exact area of western New York that Norm knew so well.

Maltbie Davenport Babcock (1858—1901) was a popular young minister in the village of Lockport, and his favorite getaway was to enjoy walking the local terrain. He would tell his young wife that he was "going out to see the Father's world." Babcock was also, rather secretly, a poet. After his death, his verses came out in a little book called *Thoughts for Every-Day Living*.

> This is my Father's world: I rest me in the thought
>      Of rocks and trees, of skies and seas;
> His hand the wonders wrought.

Thank You, **Creator God,** for the wonders You have wrought. Teach us to treasure and cherish, nurture and protect, Your creation, as we would a newborn babe. In the name of my Lord and Savior, Jesus Christ, amen.

# Keep the Channel Open

**Rescue the weak and the needy; deliver them from the hand of the wicked** (Psalm 82:4).

**Scripture:** Psalm 82
**Song:** "Deeper, Deeper"

Sandy Pond is a sheltered bay located due east of Lake Ontario. To access the lake, boaters must steer through a narrow channel dividing the pond from the larger body of water. Over time sediments, weeds, and debris accumulated within the channel, making it shallow and narrow. While small watercraft could get through, larger power boats and fishing vessels found it increasingly difficult to navigate through the opening. So every year the town brings in a dredger to scoop out the unwanted accumulation, clearing the channel and allowing the water to run deep and wide once again.

In our reading today, a warning comes to those who would disrupt and choke off access to the truth and righteousness of God. While the psalmist directs his words to the leaders of Israel, the message applies to each of us who bear the name of the Lord. One day God will come and judge the earth, dredging up and casting off offenders.

Left undisturbed, sin becomes like waterway debris, choking off access to God. By repentance, we excavate offenses as they occur, ensuring a wide channel of communication with God.

**Heavenly Father,** I give You thanks for providing a means of open communication between us through the sacrifice of Your Son for my sins. Through Christ, amen.

September 7–13. **Judyann Grant,** of Mannsville, New York, writes an inspirational column that appears in four secular newspapers.

# Clear Vision, Going Forward

**Test me, Lord, and try me, examine my heart and my mind** (Psalm 26:2).

**Scripture:** Psalm 26
**Song:** "Day by Day"

In our farmhouse we have 35 windows. The smallest, two dormers, measure a mere 20 inches across. The largest—a picture window in the living room—measures a whopping expanse of nine feet. The remainder of the windows fall somewhere in between. Along with the windows we have five doors, each with varying amounts of glass.

I love seeing the sun shine through all the windows on cloudless days, but it takes work. The windows don't clean themselves, despite advertisements that make window cleaning look like a breeze. If I tried to tackle them all in one day, the task would be overwhelming. So I break up the chore into manageable increments. As I wash each pane, cleaning away dust and cobwebs, I think ahead to the beautiful view that's coming.

Becoming Christlike doesn't come easy or naturally, either. There is no way to become more loving, faithful, and kind in one day. It takes daily commitment, being faithful in big and small matters, and living each moment with Heaven in mind.

Washing a few windows each day helps me stay on task. So, too, walking daily in faith with God helps me better handle the big challenges and tough choices that always come along.

**Dear Lord,** I long to walk close to You every day. Speak to my heart, and help me daily to keep the windows of my heart sparkling clean so that Your love might shine through me to others. I ask this in Christ's name. Amen.

# The Lure of Gossip

**Give the enemy no opportunity for slander** (1 Timothy 5:14).

**Scripture:** 1 Timothy 5:11-19
**Song:** "Holy Spirit, Be My Guide"

As I waited in the checkout line, my eyes scanned the large selection of impulse buy items that lined both sides of the aisle: candy bars, gum, breath mints, beef jerky, mini-flashlights, and batteries. Taking up the most space, however, were a variety of celebrity magazines. Each cover abounded in full-color photographs and large headlines declaring news.

Randomly, I flipped one of them open, and it contained lots of photos of celebs in less-than-flattering attire. These were accompanied by articles that were nothing more than gossip and innuendo. Disgusted, I stuffed the magazine back into the rack.

The lure of gossip began when the serpent in Eden's garden first spread distorted information about God's command. After thousands of years, gossip remains one of the ways Satan sows discord among believers. I, myself, have been guilty of trying to disguise it as a legitimate prayer concern.

As we kids headed out the door each morning, our father's parting advice was, "Keep your nose clean." That is, don't go poking it into others' business. It's still good advice. By looking well to our own affairs, we have no time to spread rumors that only cause heartache.

**Lord God,** I realize that gossip is a pothole along the pathway into which any of us can fall. But may the Holy Spirit bring my every thought, word, and deed into submission with Your will and Your plan for my life. In Your name I pray. Amen.

# Foxhole Religion?

**When you spread out your hands in prayer, I hide my eyes from you; even when you offer many prayers, I am not listening** (Isaiah 1:15).

**Scripture:** Isaiah 1:15-18
**Song:** "Just a Closer Walk with Thee"

Sitting in the dentist chair, waiting for my twice-yearly cleaning, I look at the tray of metal instruments waiting close by. While the dental hygienist pulls on rubber gloves, I pray she will find no cavities. As she picks up the sharp-pointed, double-bladed hand scaler, I silently vow to floss daily and never let decadent sweets touch my lips—ever again!

Within an hour the ordeal is over, and I'm on my way home. In less time than it takes to say "come back in six months," I have brewed a cup of enamel-staining tea and opened a bag of cavity-causing chocolates. My dentist-chair prayer? Forgotten.

Weren't the people of Judea like that? When their land was laid waste by their enemies, they desperately pleaded for God to save them. They offered sacrifices while their hearts remained distant. And they constantly returned to old, rebellious ways.

God wants our whole hearts, but not just in times of trouble. He knows when we're sincere. He desires that we settle the matter, once and for all: If we are not for Him, we are against Him. Without a complete turning away from wrongdoing, our "foxhole" prayers won't even hit the ceiling.

**Dear Father in Heaven,** I know old habits die hard, but I also know that, with an honest commitment, great change is possible. Please help me to change any attitude or action that isn't pleasing in Your sight. In Jesus' name I pray. Amen.

# Steadfast Faith

**Do not be anxious about anything, but in every situation, by prayer and petition, with thanksgiving, present your requests to God** (Philippians 4:6).

**Scripture:** Philippians 4:1-14
**Song:** "Jesus Is Lord of All"

On this anniversary of the attack on the World Trade Center, my thoughts travel back to that day. I had just gotten our first grandchild down for a nap when my husband called from work. His words tumbled out, "Have you heard? Turn on the television." As the picture came into view, I saw the south tower exploding into a cascade of fire and smoke. Tears filled my eyes as I feared war had been declared on our country.

I looked at the peaceful, sleeping form of our baby granddaughter. What kind of world had she been born into? Would she even have the opportunity to grow up? The uncertainties threatened to overwhelm me, and I turned to prayer. During those dark and somber days, and many bleak days since, Philippians 4:6 sustained me.

Two years ago our family visited the 9-11 Memorial. The hustle and bustle of the city faded away, until only the waterfall was heard. Tears again filled my eyes as, together with my now teenage granddaughter, we read the names of those who lost their lives. Our grandchildren are inheriting a broken world, but they have a loving Father who can calm their uncertainties.

**Father God,** help me remember that You will never abandon or forsake me in this imperfect world. May I keep my eyes on You and not just on my circumstances today. In Your Holy name, I offer my thanks. Amen.

# Stealing the Glory?

I baptize you with water. But one who is more powerful than I will come . . . He will baptize you with the Holy Spirit and fire (Luke 3:16).

**Scripture:** Luke 3:10-16
**Song:** "Give Him the Glory"

"Look what the rooster did!" our young visitor exclaimed. Rita held two warm brown eggs in her small hands. "He left these in the box!" The little girl had never been around chickens before. When she entered the coop, Billy, our big, red rooster, was standing in a nesting box, flapping his wings and crowing loudly. When Billy saw her, he jumped out of the box and ran out the door—like a big "chicken." That's when Rita saw the eggs in the nest.

When we fail to acknowledge the Lord's working in our lives, we mislead people into believing that our accomplishments happen by our own efforts. We bask in the praise of people instead of giving the glory to God.

John the Baptist was neither imposter nor chicken. A popular preacher, he proclaimed Christ at every turn. He knew Jesus was the real thing. When people wondered if John were the promised messiah, he set them straight. He used every opportunity to proclaim Christ—eventually at the cost of his life.

I wonder how it is for God when He sees us running around, crowing about our accomplishments, stealing His glory.

**Father God,** forgive me when I take credit for what You have done in my life. Take away any foolish pride in me, that I may give You all the glory. In Your precious name I ask. Amen.

# Share Your Resources

**From time to time those who owned land or houses sold them, brought the money from the sales and put it at the apostles' feet, and it was distributed to anyone who had need** (Acts 4:34, 35).

**Scripture:** Acts 4:34—5:10
**Song:** "Make Me a Blessing"

Our church donates items to our community's Friendship Shop. The volunteer-operated store sells the items and uses the money to aid folks facing financial hardship. It's a win-win situation as our trash becomes someone's treasure.

When I did my September spring cleaning, I tossed several items into a pile to donate. One was a flannel shirt my husband had never worn—and with good reason. The gaudy shirt was covered with large black and yellow checks. It looked like something a lumberjack would wear.

A few weeks later, when it came time to dress my autumn scarecrow, I made a quick stop at the Friendship Shop. I found a perfect shirt and plunked down two dollars for it.

When my husband came home, he thought Mr. Scarecrow looked quite dapper in the black and yellow-checked shirt. He laughed when I told him I had given it away, only to buy it back. But after all, the whole idea of the thrift store is to raise money to help those in need. When I put the scarecrow away for the winter, I again donated the shirt. And now that autumn is coming, I just may check to see if the shirt is still there.

**God,** I give thanks for people who work to help those in need. May I always do what I can to help ease the financial burdens of others. In Jesus' name, amen.

# A Love Song, but Not Silly

**Your throne, O God, endures forever and ever. You rule with a scepter of justice"** (Psalm 45:6, *New Living Translation*).

**Scripture:** Psalm 45:1-7
**Song:** "O, How I Love Jesus"

I couldn't get the Paul McCartney tune out of my head that talked about people who wanted to fill the world with "silly love songs" and asks "What's wrong with that?"

For one thing, it was annoying. McCartney is singing a silly love song about silly loves songs. But he does answer the question, "What's wrong with that?" (Answer: "Love isn't silly").
So the question is answered and explained. That's the basic flow of McCartney's silly lyrics. Yet there's really no need to *explain* when we sing our love songs to God, as the psalmist did. He uses the king as an example, because the king is God's servant. In the New Testament, Hebrews 1:8, 9 quotes Psalm 45:6, referring to Christ.

Have you written a love song lately? Or at least sung one in your heart? A Bible study teacher I know suggested that we pause regularly during our day and lift up this song, "Lord, I love You." While we may not sing the words, we can at least say them. How much sweeter when we say them as a sincere prayer.

**Lord God,** words cannot express my love for You. My heart truly overflows, and so do my tears of joy for knowing You. Thank You for first loving me! I pray this prayer in the name of Jesus, my Savior and Lord. Amen.

September 14–20. **Jimmie Oliver Fleming** is enjoying her new home and new neighbors, where she lives and writes in Chester, Virginia.

# Ruled by Anger . . . or No Regrets?

**People with understanding control their anger; a hot temper shows great foolishness** (Proverbs 14:29, *New Living Translation*).

**Scripture:** Proverbs 14:22-29
**Song:** "Love Lifted Me"

Many tragedies have occurred because of a hasty temper. And I can vouch for that, firsthand. Yet in some cases, my hasty temper can be rightly directed toward me, Jimmie. For instance, I've never forgotten the time when I let a gem of an opportunity slip away because I thought it was "too good to be true." Now I get angry every time I think about it, because moving forward on this wonderful opportunity could have saved me a lot of money and a lot of trouble too. That anger is good motivation to learn and to do better next time.

The old saying "Don't cry over spilled milk" has to overcome my constant regret, though, if I'm to move forward with joy. I'm learning to hand the past over to the Lord.

Bottom line: Thank the Lord for second chances.

And third and fourth chances too! And fifth and sixth.

Well, I think you get the idea. We might need to let anger do its work in us for a season. Then we simply must find ways to let it go. Usually, the best way is to take all that pent-up energy and—rather than directing it at a *person*—point it like a laser beam at a *problem* to be solved.

**O God**, I'm so thankful that You are in control of all the circumstances in my life, especially my anger. Thank You for lifting me in love. Nothing else could have helped. Having tried other methods, I know this for sure! In Jesus' name, amen.

# Home Sweet Home

**Jesus returned to Galilee in the power of the Spirit, and news about him spread through the whole countryside** (Luke 4:14).

**Scripture:** Luke 4:14-19
**Song:** "Jubilee"

A long day at the office can often make you utter the words "home sweet home." Yet in some instances, you may dread going home. What if you don't get the welcome you expect? Or what if you're greeted by the ton of work you left behind? Or how about having to face the guests who came visiting? (On that note, it has been said that the one thing you should never tell your guests is "make yourselves at home").

Unlike us, Jesus was prepared for all circumstances. Before arriving in Nazareth, His boyhood home, He'd become well known throughout the surrounding country. His time of teaching in the synagogue brought praise from everyone. And He continued teaching in His hometown, proclaiming the good news to an enslaved and downtrodden people.

Like Jesus, we can be instruments of spreading good news. There are so many enslaved and downtrodden people around us today, in any hometown! (Think of the addicted—or the financially struggling.)

We are expected to give as Jesus did. We've received redemption, release from captivity to all lesser gods. Now we can be a light of God's grace in our hometown, and everywhere we go.

Thank You, **Father,** for sending Your Son to make it possible for us to be at home with You for eternity someday. May we show others the way "home" also. Amen.

# Run for Your Life!

**Pursue righteous living, faithfulness, love, and peace. Enjoy the companionship of those who call on the Lord with pure hearts** (2 Timothy 2:22, *New Living Translation*).

**Scripture:** 2 Timothy 2:14-16, 22-26
**Song:** "More Like the Master"

There's a time to stand still and a time to run. Depending on the circumstances, you may find yourself literally running for your life. However, if you are in the presence of those with impure hearts, this would also qualify for a time to run. It can be the case, whether you're young or old.

I have had to run or stand still by not making a particular phone call. In other cases, I have phoned friends and gotten their answering machines and have been highly thankful that I did. Listening to their greeting message gives me a way out. And if I leave a message at all, I make sure that it's a positive one, and one that reflects the principles in our Scripture today.

For example, I'll say, "Hi, Leticia. I'm just checking to see how you and John are doing. Have a great day." Another time I might say, "Oh, hello, Mrs. White. Sorry I missed you. I just wanted to say 'Happy Thursday morning.'"

Pursuing faith, love, and peace truly works. When you do so from the beginning, you're less likely to have to run for your life. (Still, I think it's a good idea to keep those running shoes handy.)

**Lord,** thank You for Your Word. Thank You that Your thoughts are not my thoughts, as the prophet Isaiah proclaimed. Yet I know I can remove my impure thoughts with Your help! Through Jesus my Savior, I pray. Amen.

# Stopping the Curse

**No longer will there be a curse upon anything. For the throne of God and of the Lamb will be there, and his servants will worship him** (Revelation 22:3, *New Living Translation*).

**Scripture:** Revelation 22:1-7
**Song:** "Follow the Lamb"

One definition of "curse" involves the ideas of *pain* and *trouble.* A certain home on the market was said to be cursed, so the real estate agent decided to pass on that one. Besides, she had an inkling that word had gotten around and that house would probably be on the market for a long time.

On the other hand, she knew from experience that the house she had finally landed as her own dream home had been on the market for five years. Even though newly built and conveniently located by two major interstates—and dozens of area merchants—no one had ever purchased it. She had decided that it was just meant for her.

However, she soon changed her mind. Lots of repairs were needed—so the house was actually a pain. She couldn't stop this pain (or curse), however; she simply had to live with it.

Down here on earth, we all have to live with a certain amount of daily pain and trouble. Yet in Heaven, we'll have no more curse, no more pain, no more trouble. Let us follow the Lamb now, so we'll be perfectly comfortable living with Him in eternity.

**O God,** I've experienced much pain and trouble and suffering in this world. Yet I know You have prepared a better place for me. Worshipping You faithfully down here means worshipping You always in Heaven. Thank You, in Jesus' name, amen.

# A Name That Really Counts

**Salvation is found in no one else, for there is no other name under heaven given to mankind by which we must be saved** (Acts 4:12).

**Scripture:** Acts 4:5-12
**Song:** "The Name of Jesus"

"What is your nickname?" a man once asked me. "I'm just curious." I wouldn't share it with him (nor with you!). My real name, Jimmie, is more important.

In fact, names, in general, are very important. This applies to the brands of the things we buy for our households. For example, some people will buy only name brand products. Nothing else will do.

And consider the famous celebrity names. Many are instantly recognizable, even as first names only. Oprah, for example, means only one person in your mind, right?

But what about the rest of us, with no name recognition? Or whose names have questionable reputations attached to them?

Jesus came to give hope to such people. This is why His name is above all other names, even on the refrigerator. My granddaughters Yelena and Ngozi illustrated this one day when they rearranged some magnets on my refrigerator, making sure the one with the name Jesus on it went at the top.

That name will remain permanently affixed on my refrigerator. What a glorious name to remember each day!

Thank You, **dear Jesus,** for being my Savior. How blessed I am to be able to claim Your name. I know that only You can save me. And only You can keep me safe, now and forever. Thank You, once again, in Your precious name. Amen.

# Rejoicing in Suffering

**The apostles left the Sanhedrin, rejoicing because they had been counted worthy of suffering disgrace for the Name** (Acts 5:41).

**Scripture:** Acts 5:27-29, 33-42
**Song:** "Were You There When They Crucified My Lord?"

Peter and the other apostles set an example for moving forward in faith and witness for the Lord. They even rejoiced in the disgrace that came to them for bearing Jesus' name—and believed that suffering for Him was somehow a badge of worthiness in God's eyes. It mattered not what the world thought of them. They rejoiced and continued to teach every day, publicly as well as in their homes.

Hopefully I will take hold of this example and do more teaching in my home. Some of my family members are quick to criticize me for my beliefs (and I do suffer for this). However, I know that they need to hear the all-important and life-saving message, "The one you are looking for is Jesus."

When I think of the troubles and sufferings any of us disciples will encounter because of our faith, I recall some words of a famous nineteenth-century minister, Henry Ward Beecher. May they bless you, as well: "Affliction comes to us all, not to make us sad, but sober; not to make us sorry, but to make us wise; not to make us despondent, but by its darkness to refresh us as the night refreshes the day."

**Heavenly Father,** thank You for keeping me strong when so many things try to creep in and get me offtrack in my service to You. I know that I can go through whatever is necessary, and even rejoice, through Your strength. In Jesus' name, I pray. Amen.

# God Keeps Covenant

**The LORD your God, He is God, the faithful God, who keeps His covenant and His lovingkindness to a thousandth generation with those who love Him and keep His commandments** (Deuteronomy 7:9, *New American Standard Bible*).

**Scripture:** Deuteronomy 7:1-11
**Song:** "Ah, Lord God"

The man came out of Vietnam wounded in body and soul, crushed in every way. He, like Ishmael, was a wild man—against everyone, with everyone against him. No one could speak to him about God without being cursed by him. One day, while on his motorcycle, he was hit by a huge truck. His body was now as mangled as his heart; he would never walk again.

As I sat by Bush's bedside, I prayed, "Lord, give me the words You would say." I began, "There were two men on crosses beside Jesus. They were not religious, they didn't know any theology, never studied Scripture. One cursed Jesus, and one asked to be with Him in paradise. That second man is you, Bush. Only now it is God who is calling *you* to be with *Him*." I went on to tell him that God didn't care so much about his past as what he would decide about his future. Would he trust God with it?

I had prayed many years for my brother Bush. And that day he became a child of my covenant-keeping God.

Thanks, **Lord,** that You keep covenant with Your children. You have been faithful to my family and me from generation to generation. Praise You, in the name of Jesus, Lord and Savior of all. Amen.

September 21–27. **Marty Prudhomme,** of Mandeville, Louisiana, is a mom, grandmother, and great-grandmother. She teaches Bible studies and leads an evangelism ministry called Adopt a Block.

# No Disappointment Here

**Incline Your ear to me, rescue me quickly; be to me a rock of strength, a stronghold to save me** (Psalm 31:2, *New American Standard Bible*).

**Scripture:** Psalm 31:1-5, 19-24
**Song:** "Praise You in This Storm"

At 13 years of age, Michelle suddenly fell into a coma. Her family was devastated to learn she had fluid on the brain. The doctors didn't know why it happened, but they quickly inserted a drain tube to relieve the pressure.

The family began a prayer vigil in Michelle's hospital room, asking friends to help. I too sat with her and prayed Psalm 31 aloud each time I would visit. Her parents and I prayed many times, "Lord, in You we have taken refuge, incline Your ear and rescue Michelle. She is Your child; we put our hope in You."

Two months passed, and then Michelle suddenly woke up. She immediately began to sit up, talk, and walk with very little help. It seemed to us that God had fought her battle when she wasn't able to help herself. Today Michelle is a wife and mother with children of her own.

Often we find ourselves in situations that are totally out of our control. We feel helpless and may become frustrated. These are perfect opportunities for us to trust the Lord. God will be a stronghold for those who call on His name and place their trust in Him. I firmly believe He will not disappoint us.

**King of glory,** I put my trust in You. You are my rock of strength. Help me to be strong and courageous, even when things look hopeless. In the holy name of Jesus, my Lord and Savior, I pray. Amen.

# My Delight

**If Your law had not been my delight, then I would have perished in my affliction** (Psalm 119:92, *New American Standard Bible*).

**Scripture:** Psalm 119:89-94
**Song:** "Thy Word Is a Lamp unto My Feet"

The love of my life had grown cold—I wanted a divorce. He and I were very different, we clashed at every turn, and the fighting seemed endless. Things would certainly be difficult, and my prayer was, "Lord, please don't let this hurt my children."

A group of ladies at my church were praying for me and invited me to their Bible study. I'd never been to a Bible study, so I was willing to see what it was all about. The ladies showed me how to study the Word for myself—and it was so exciting and challenging to discover God's will for my life. Soon I began to realize what God was saying about marriage in the Scriptures.

I'd prayed for an easy divorce (as if there were such a thing). Instead, God gave me a hunger for His will and taught me to trust in His ways. He revived my love for my husband as I walked in obedience to biblical precepts.

All of this happened 40 years ago. My husband and I have been married now for 45 years, and I have never regretted following God's plan. When we surrender to Him, He revitalizes parts of our lives that we'd thought were lost forever.

**Almighty and most merciful God,** You are full of lovingkindness and patience. I would have been lost and unhappy in my affliction without Your precepts. Please continue to teach me Your Word and give me grace to keep Your commands. In the precious name of Jesus I pray. Amen.

## God Equips Us

**In everything you were enriched in Him, in all speech and all knowledge** (1 Corinthians 1:5, *New American Standard Bible*).

**Scripture:** 1 Corinthians 1:1-9
**Song:** "You Raise Me Up"

My husband, Bill, is an electrical engineer and computer specialist. He's your guy for any kind of technical job. When Bill gave his life to the Lord, he worried about how God could possibly use his abilities. He would ask me, "I can't preach, teach Bible studies, or sing. How can I be of use to the Lord?"

Bill soon discovered that God had already equipped him with every gift he needed. His first opportunity to use his talents came when Bill met a minister in our community who was building a church. The minister was in a financial bind and asked Bill to design the wiring for his church. Since that time, Bill has developed church websites, designed sound systems, and planned various types of audio/video setups for Christian ministries and missionaries.

At one large church he developed a video ministry, even training the volunteers in using the cameras. Singers and teachers abound, but very few people have Bill's much-needed skills.

Many of us may wonder, "How can God use me?" Through his letters to the Corinthians, Paul reassures us that God has given each church what it needs to grow and thrive. Each of us has a spiritual gift to contribute to the cause.

**Dear God,** thank You for equipping our churches with the spiritual gifts we need to serve You and one another. I ask that You would continue to use me for Your glory, as I eagerly await Your glorious return. Through Christ, amen.

# Another Opportunity to Trust?

**Examine everything carefully; hold fast to that which is good** (1 Thessalonians 5:21, *New American Standard Bible*).

**Scripture:** 1 Thessalonians 5:16-25
**Song:** "Rejoice in the Lord Always"

The doctor said I would be like "the guy on the golf course" — who dies quickly from a heart attack. Surprisingly, I wasn't frightened, because the Lord whispered to me in a still small voice, "You are in a win–win situation." If I died, it would be quick. And if I lived, it would be God's will. I thought to myself, "win–win." I was amazed that I could rejoice in the Lord.

There were three choices: quench the Spirit, panic, or choose to rejoice and give thanks that God's will ruled over my life. In fact, I found tremendous comfort in knowing God would make the final decision. Rejoicing lifted my spirit and calmed my emotions.

Fifteen years have passed since that time, and my heart is ticking just fine, perfectly normal for my age. The Lord taught me to listen to His voice, to examine everything carefully, and to cling to what is good.

I suppose it always comes down to trust or don't trust, doesn't it? We face difficult choices daily. We can receive God's wisdom and peace or refuse it. The thing is, it takes practice to learn how to put our full weight in His arms. Maybe that's why He allows the constant procession of opportunities to do it.

**Dear Lord,** give me a greater sensitivity to Your Word, and help me yield to Your will. Teach me to trust more. I want to cling to what is good and continually rejoice in Your goodness. I pray in the name of Jesus my Lord. Amen.

# Full of Grace and Power

**Stephen, a man full of God's grace and power, performed great wonders and signs among the people** (Acts 6:8).

**Scripture:** Acts 6:7-15
**Song:** "No Chains on Me"

My friends Gail and Greg were American missionaries working in various churches in Costa Rica. The power of the gospel message was spreading, and the Lord's signs and wonders became evident to many people. On the front lines of the gospel's advance, when the message would encounter pagan beliefs or even demonic influence, it seemed the Lord worked in special ways. There were physical healings, for instance, and many new churches sprang up overnight.

However, before long, some ministers became jealous of the churches that were growing. Lies began to spread, saying Gail and Greg were false teachers. Eventually the leadership of the churches called them in to accuse them. This action hurt Gail and Greg deeply, but they didn't argue with the leaders; instead, they trusted the Lord to defend them.

One by one, the lies of their accusers came to light. The couple continued to minister in Costa Rica, Panama, and Guatemala. My friends were not the only ministers to experience the revival that swept Costa Rica and most of Central America in the 1970s and 80s. When God's Word is preached—the kingdom of God increases.

**O Lord,** You are my Savior, Redeemer, and healer. I pray that You will use me to bring the good news of Your gospel to many people. I want to follow You and be a witness to others of Your great love and goodness. I pray in Jesus' name. Amen.

# He'll Rescue You

**[God] rescued him from all his troubles. He gave Joseph wisdom and enabled him to gain the goodwill of Pharaoh . . . So Pharaoh made him ruler over Egypt** (Acts 7:10).

**Scripture:** Acts 7:2-4, 8-10, 17, 33, 34, 45-47, 52, 53
**Song:** "My Deliverer"

The Lord rescued my grandson Scott by sending him to prison. He was a drug user who became a dealer in order to pay for his habit. But while in jail, he fully committed his life to the Lord and was healed from many old wounds.

Scott learned obedience to the Lord through many trials as he remained in prison. He worked diligently to get a welding certificate, took two years of business college, and gained a sign-language certificate. Soon he moved into the deaf dormitory where he led many prisoners to the Lord and helped others with their paroles.

Scott was greatly persecuted for his faith, but he found favor with the warden, his teachers, and many ministries in the prison community. God heard his groans and the prayers of his family. He gave Scott favor in the midst of his own personal Egypt. Yesterday Scott phoned; he was with his Gramps on the way home. They wanted to surprise me—he'd been released three months early. And the man who'd taught him sign language is the translator for the governor of Louisiana. He has a job waiting for Scott.

**Dear Lord,** You have seen my oppression, heard my prayers, and rescued me out of the hand of my enemies. You are my deliverer and have shown me great favor. I pray for Your continued protection. In Jesus' name. Amen.

# The Guest List

**LORD, who may abide in Your tabernacle? Who may dwell in Your holy hill?** (Psalm 15:1, *New King James Version*).

**Scripture:** Psalm 15
**Song:** "More Holiness Give Me"

Our granddaughter was making a list of family, friends, and coworkers for her wedding. She pictured the people as she wrote their names. The guest list grew as she thought of the people who had been a part of her life for 22 years. Customers she waited on weekly, at the restaurant, were also included.

Her fiancé had a list, but there were some questionable people on it from his past years, before he'd become a Christian. They decided to invite those with good character, not those who were known for questionable behaviors or causing dissension.

The details of the wedding were meticulously planned, the right colors blending with the theme set by the bride. She wanted everything to be as perfect as possible. On her wedding day, she would be transformed from the friendly waitress to the beautiful bride.

I want to be on the guest list of the Lord and be a person of good character. What is a person of good character? David gives us the answer in this short psalm. Won't you join me in taking it to heart today?

**Lord,** thank You for showing me what's required to be on Your guest list. Help me to have a strong, good character. I want to dwell with You in eternity. I seek to please You in my days on earth. Guide me, in Jesus' name. Amen.

September 28–30. **Beverly LaHote Schwind** retired to Tennessee and teaches at a rehab mission. She is the author of five books, as well as being a Senior Olympics medalist.

# One Life

**Keep your lives free from the love of money and be content with what you have, because God has said, "Never will I leave you; never will I forsake you"** (Hebrews 13:5).

**Scripture:** Hebrews 13:5-10
**Song:** "Unsearchable Riches"

Charles Thomas Studd, known as C. T. Studd, became a Christian when he was 18 years old in 1878. This wealthy young man attended Trinity College in Cambridge, England. He ended his school career in a blaze of glory as a cricket player (still considered best in the world). Fame shadowed his commitment to Christ until his brother became very ill. This caused C. T. to realize how unimportant fame, glory, and wealth were.

He stunned the world by leaving it all behind, and with a passion became one of the "Cambridge Seven" that followed a missionary calling to China in 1885. His motto was: "If Jesus is God and He died for me, then there is no sacrifice too great for me to make for Him."

This makes me think of the rich young ruler in Luke 18. Jesus told this young man to sell all he had and distribute it to the poor; he would have treasure in Heaven. Then Jesus invited the man to follow Him. But the man couldn't bring himself to give his possessions away, as he was very rich. He allowed his treasures to keep him from following Christ (see Luke 18:18-23).

But what did C. T. Studd say? "Only one life, 'twill soon be past. Only what's done for Christ will last."

**Dear Lord,** thank You for the blessings I enjoy in my life. Help me to control my finances and not let them control me. In Jesus' name, amen.

# Hunting Season

**Take the helmet of salvation, and the sword of the Spirit, which is the word of God** (Ephesians 6:17, *New King James Version*).

**Scripture:** Ephesians 6:14-18
**Song:** "God's Got an Army"

"Where's my hunting vest?" I heard my husband mumble to himself as he and our son organized their equipment. Our son had come from out of state to go hunting with his dad. Neither of them had ever gone turkey hunting before, but they'd talked about it for a few years and read much about it. Now they'd been invited to hunt on a wooded property.

I took pictures of them. They had on their hunting hats, camouflaged vests, buckled up boots. They had their ammunition belted, and they carried their guns. "It looks like you're going to war," I said as I snapped the picture.

"We are, against the turkeys," they laughed.

Spiritual battles need their equipment too. We can equip ourselves in the same manner as the hunter or soldier—but against the spiritual forces of darkness. The spoken Word of God, empowered by the Holy Spirit, will help attract the sincere seeker of truth. Also, when we have our armor on, we can stand against all manner of fiery temptations.

I'm not good at memorizing, so I write encouraging Scriptures on index cards, and I put them on my refrigerator door. Thus I "put on" God's Word, and it becomes my daily armor.

**Dear Father,** I thank You for Your Word. As I dress each day, I want to be reminded to put on that special armor You have provided. In Jesus' name, amen.

# My Prayer Notes

# DEVOTIONS®

**OCTOBER**

The righteous are as bold as a lion.

*—Proverbs 28:1*

**Gary Wilde,** Editor　　**Margaret Williams,** Project Editor　　　　Photo Blend Images | Thinkstock©

*DEVOTIONS®* is published quarterly by Standard Publishing, Cincinnati, Ohio, www.standardpub.com.
© 2014 by Standard Publishing. All rights reserved. Topics based on the Home Daily Bible Readings,
International Sunday School Lessons. © 2012 by the Committee on the Uniform Series. Printed in
the U.S.A. All Scripture quotations, unless otherwise indicated, are taken from the *HOLY BIBLE,*
*NEW INTERNATIONAL VERSION®*. *NIV®*. Copyright © 1973, 1978, 1984, 2011 by Biblica, Inc.®
Used by permission of Zondervan. All rights reserved worldwide. *New American Standard Bible®*,
*(NASB)* Copyright © 1960, 1962, 1963, 1968, 1971, 1972, 1973, 1975, 1977, 1995 by The Lock-
man Foundation. Used by permission. (www.Lockman.org). *Holy Bible, New Living Translation*
*(NLT)*, © 1996, 2004, 2007. Tyndale House Publishers. Scripture quotations marked *(NKJV)* are
taken from the *New King James Version®*. Copyright © 1982 by Thomas Nelson, Inc. Used by
permission. All rights reserved. *The Living Bible (TLB)*, © 1971 by Tyndale House Publishers,
Wheaton, IL.

# Joy in the Cottage

**The disciples were filled with joy and with the Holy Spirit** (Acts 13:52, *New King James Version*).

**Scripture:** Acts 13:52–14:3
**Song:** "Jesus Saves"

"Jim, can you meet me at the Sullivan cottage? I'm working there tomorrow morning." The phone call was from my husbands' friend Stan, who was struggling with some problems in his life. Jim had advised Stan at times in the past, also sharing how his own life had changed after his baptism into Christ.

Stan and Jim spent the morning in the empty cottage, talking things over. Stan wanted some changes in his life. They shared and prayed, and then Stan asked the Lord to forgive him and come into his life. It happened 25 years ago, and they still talk about it with great joy. In fact, Stan gets teary every time he talks about the day in the cottage story.

The bond between these two men is strong even though they live states apart. A marriage was saved—and other issues handled—when Jesus was invited into the situation.

Telling someone about the Lord is exciting, but sometimes we may just plant the seed of faith, knowing that someone else will actually witness the results. This brings joy to the messenger and the convert. It is a joy that lasts—an everlasting joy.

**Lord,** thank You for the joy that comes into our hearts when we tell others about Your plan of salvation for them. Nothing else can measure up to that joy! In Christ, amen.

October 1–4. **Beverly LaHote Schwind** retired to Tennessee and teaches at a rehabilitation mission. She is the author of five books, as well as being a Senior Olympics medalist.

# Joy in the City

**The believers who had fled Jerusalem went everywhere preaching the Good News about Jesus!** (Acts 8:4, *The Living Bible*).

**Scripture:** Acts 8:1-8
**Song:** "I Love to Tell the Story"

"It's a boy!" I watched on TV as joy spread through the city of London. Kate and William, the Duke and Duchess of Cambridge, had a baby boy. When the couple first arrived at the hospital, the crowd waited outside for hours to be the first to hear the news. The media waited with the crowd, interviewing various people and repeating the same reports over and over.

It was good news that an heir to the throne was born, healthy and whole. And that news rippled through the world in myriad languages.

There was other news that week, news of disaster to airlines and forest fires raging in the West. But the good news of what had happened in England seemed to take priority. Well-wishers went back to their homes and countries full of joy. They will pass the story to future generations: *We were at the hospital the day the prince was born!*

The believers who heard about Jesus left Jerusalem, and their joy was much greater than their fear. They had witnessed miracles, and they couldn't contain what they'd seen and heard. That's just how it is when the world changes for the better.

**Jesus**, I pray that the good news of Your birth and resurrection be proclaimed to the world. Fill me, Lord, so that I may share this message with others and tell of Your goodness in my life. In Jesus' name I pray. Amen.

# What a Trough!

**Then Phillip said, "If you believe with all your heart, you may." And he answered and said, "I believe that Jesus Christ is the Son of God"** (Acts 8:37, *New King James Version*).

**Scripture:** Acts 8:26-40
**Song:** "Come, Now Is the Time to Worship"

Nine girls in orange scrubs walked into the jail garage. Their faces showed fear, anxiety . . . and yet . . . there was an air of excitement. White towels draped about the necks of some, while others clutched their towels like a pacifier.

A large metal trough for watering animals stood in the middle of the room, and the minister stood waiting to baptize the women and then the men. They'd given their hearts to Christ.

The guards stood at the door as the names of the women rang out. No choir sang as they walked forward. Having been taught week after week about the love of Jesus, they had said, like the eunuch, "I believe and want to be baptized." Next, the group of men that had also asked to be baptized came into the garage and nervously awaited their turns.

I thought about how Christ was born and laid in a feeding trough. And now these men and women in jail were baptized into His family . . . in a watering trough. As their teachers, we applauded them all and hugged each one, grateful to be a part of their entrance into the kingdom of God.

**Dear Jesus,** thank You for the gift of eternal life through baptism! As Phillip brought understanding of Your salvation to the eunuch, help me to shine forth Your saving love in all I do and say. I am so grateful for Your mercy and grace. In Your holy name I pray. Amen.

# Real or Fake?

**Peter said to him, "May your silver perish with you, because you thought you could obtain the gift of God with money!"** (Acts 8:20, *New American Standard Bible*).

**Scripture:** Acts 8:9-24
**Song:** "All Who, with Heart Confiding"

When I was 12, I was baptized with a class of others, because that is how they did it in my church. Everyone presumed that I knew who Jesus was, and I thought I did too. I received a Bible, a cross, and a certificate.

I thought I was a Christian. I sang all the songs and sat in church almost every Sunday. From my outward appearance I *was* a Christian. I went to Bible camp when I was in my teens and saw a passion in people that I did not have. Many of them were thrilled with reading the Bible.

I was hungry for what they had, and finally I was able to hear with my heart what the Lord was saying through the good teachers around me. I suppose I could say the Holy Spirit ministered to me; I do know that Jesus became real to me.

Any of us could buy a T-shirt with a Christian emblem on it. We might purchase a beautiful silver cross and wear it every day. We may look the part, but none of this would produce a genuine faith. Faith is a matter of the heart—not merchandise. In other words, the stark message of Peter to Simon is applicable to us today.

**Dear Lord,** thank You for the free gift of salvation that You offer to all people. You alone were able to purchase it—with precious drops of Your own blood. In light of Your great sacrifice, I wish to give my whole life to You. In Jesus' name, amen.

# Really Clean?

**The LORD has rewarded me according to my righteousness, according to the cleanness of my hands in his sight** (Psalm 18:24).

**Scripture:** Psalm 18:20-30
**Song:** "Cleanse Me"

Training my 2-year-old son to wash his hands has been an adventure. Usually he's more interested in splashing the water out of the sink than onto his hands. I let him participate in the process, but I help him scrub his chubby digits to make sure they actually get clean. Even though I'm doing most of the work, I lavish praise on my little guy for a job well done.

God rewards those whose hands are clean in His sight. As Christians, we know we're saved by God's grace, not by works (see Ephesians 2:8, 9). When we receive that gift of salvation, God sees Christ's righteousness in us rather than our sin. Our hearts and hands are not yet fully clean on their own—they are soiled by our sin—though the process of cleansing has begun. But they are clean in His sight, purified by Jesus' blood.

What a loving heavenly Father we serve! Even we, as sinners, know how to give good gifts to our children. How much more gracious is our God for cleansing us through the blood of His Son and by the work of His Spirit in our hearts.

**Lord,** thank You for justifying grace, Your declaration of righteousness. And thank You for the sanctifying process of cleansing that continues in me daily. One day I will stand before You, perfectly clean in every way. Praise You, through Christ! Amen.

October 5–11. **Lisa Earl** writes from her home in western Pennsylvania. She enjoys spending time with her husband, two young sons, and cream tabby cat.

# A Legacy of Faith

**Surely the righteous will never be shaken; they will be remembered forever** (Psalm 112:6).

**Scripture:** Psalm 112:1, 2, 6-9
**Song:** "Faith of Our Fathers"

I've recently started making family collages for my children. Two of my grandparents and my uncle recently passed away, and I want the kids to remember these beloved family members. But when I realized I'd have to label each photo, it became a much more complicated process than I first envisioned.

Then it hit me: as our children and future grandchildren—and even our great-grandchildren—branch out on their own, these ancestors will be long forgotten, and so will I. It's inevitable. Who knows anything about their great-great-great-great grandparents? Such things are easier today with digital photography, but eventually we will all be forgotten. Only one legacy can be left behind permanently: The person of Jesus Christ, and His gracious offer of adoption into the Father's family.

My children may not know that my grandma went to church every Sunday or that her favorite hymn was "How Great Thou Art," but they will know that gospel message. They may not remember that my mom sang Vacation Bible School songs with me on the swing set, but they will know the gospel. I may not remember my great-great-great grandparents, but surely some of them loved the Lord. Their legacy of faith lives on.

**Dear God,** please help me to share Your truth with my children, grandchildren, or other young people You place in my path. May the truth of Your gospel endure from generation to generation. In Jesus' name, amen.

# Paranoia Needed?

**Since you call on a Father who judges each person's work impartially, live out your time as foreigners here in reverent fear** (1 Peter 1:17).

**Scripture:** 1 Peter 1:16-19
**Song:** "Guide Me, O Thou Great Jehovah"

My husband and I decided to spend a week in Prince Edward Island, Canada, a few years ago. As a lifelong fan of the Anne of Green Gables books, I couldn't wait for this adventure to begin.

We signed up for an official tour of the area, riding in a van with a tour guide. As we rumbled over country roads, some made only of tightly packed red dirt, I started to become a bit paranoid. Here we were, far out in the country—in a foreign country—with just our tour guide and a retired English couple. Our cell phones didn't work. We had no idea where we were going or how to get back to our inn. An uncomfortable feeling set in: We were at the mercy of this guide.

Likewise, as Christians, we are foreigners on this earth. We don't know where life will take us next. The road might be smooth for a while, but often we're led through rough patches: illness, injury, financial problems, relational conflict.

We are at the mercy of Jesus, our guide, to help us find our way back home to Him. Thankfully, we know that Jesus is a kind, gracious, perfect guide, and He will never abandon us or lead us astray. No need for the slightest paranoia.

**Dear Lord,** help me to follow You in every area of my life today. As You keep my focus on Heaven, my ultimate destination, may I be a good ambassador of Your love right here until I arrive home. In Jesus name, amen.

# The Wisdom Before Us

**The Queen of the South will rise at the judgment with the people of this generation and condemn them, for she came from the ends of the earth to listen to Solomon's wisdom; and now something greater than Solomon is here** (Luke 11:31).

**Scripture:** Luke 11:30-37
**Song:** "Eternal Wisdom, Thee We Praise"

A former university professor and gay activist recently published a book titled *The Secret Thoughts of an Unlikely Convert.* In this memoir, she writes about her conversion to Christianity after receiving a thought-provoking letter from a local minister. She sought godly wisdom by meeting with the minister and his wife in their home. After coming to Christ, she left her former community and lost many friends and colleagues.

Today's passage warns us against ignoring God's revelation. The queen of Sheba came to Solomon, the king of Israel, because she had heard of his godly wisdom. This was long before Jesus, the greatest revelation, came to earth and died on the cross for our sins.

I've gone to church all of my life, and I've believed in Jesus for as long as I can remember. I don't want to take that for granted. So I must ask myself: How am I allowing the truth of the gospel to transform my life? Am I truly seeking God's wisdom? Let us daily recognize the privilege of having the greatest wisdom right before us: the message of Christ crucified, risen, ascended, and coming again.

**Father,** thank You for the privilege of knowing You and Your Word. Help me to become more and more thankful for the precious gift of Your Son. In His name, amen.

# The Blink of an Eye

**For three days he was blind, and did not eat or drink anything** (Acts 9:9).

**Scripture:** Acts 9:1-9
**Song:** "I Waited Patient for the Lord"

Recently, Google engineers discovered that Internet users won't even wait 400 milliseconds—literally the blink of an eye—for a website to load. Software developers seek to make websites work faster and faster as people search for information from computers, smart phones, and other devices that connect to the Internet.

Today's passage tells us that Saul waited three days before he received the Holy Spirit and began preaching. After he heard the voice of the risen Jesus on the road to Damascus, he was blind and had to be led by his companions the rest of the way.

The biblical time frame of three days is powerful. Abraham was commanded to sacrifice his son, Isaac, and he set out on a three-day journey. Jonah languished in the belly of a fish for three days. Jesus rose from the dead on the third day.

Sometimes God's plan requires patience. In a culture that can't even pause for the blink of an eye, let us fix our eyes unflinchingly on Jesus, the pioneer and perfecter of our faith (see Hebrews 12:2). Then we will be able, in quietness and confidence, to discern His will for our lives. And we will be able, with wisdom and grace, to share the gospel with those He places in our paths.

**Lord Jesus,** I fix my eyes on You today. Free me from distractions, doubts, and fears. In the name of the Father and of the Son and of the Holy Spirit I pray. Amen.

# Recharging Through Fellowship

**After taking some food, he regained his strength** (Acts 9:19).

**Scripture:** Acts 9:10-19
**Song:** "What a Fellowship"

My husband and I live several hours away from our families and the friends we knew in childhood. We both moved from rural areas to a midsized city to attend college and find work. Most of our college friends left the area after graduation, leaving us feeling isolated.

A few years after we were married, we joined a church dinner group that meets in each other's homes. Each family brings a food item to share, and we simply eat and enjoy the company of friends. The four families in the group have all had children at the same time, and we now strive to raise our children in the fear and admonition of the Lord. We encourage one another.

The idea isn't all that new. The apostle Paul was the most powerful missionary in Christian history. It would make sense that, once he received the Holy Spirit, he'd jump up and immediately begin preaching. Nevertheless, he took time to eat and then spent several days with the disciples in Damascus, sharing in fellowship and gaining strength for the work ahead. He too needed the support and encouragement of other believers.

Let us never be afraid to take time simply to enjoy the fellowship of other believers. How refreshing it can be—and how essential for a powerful witness to the world around us.

**Dear Lord,** help me connect with others in Your body, the church. Place people in my path with whom I can serve, grow, and share. In Jesus' name, amen.

# Keep the Main Thing, the Main Thing

**Living in the fear of the Lord and encouraged by the Holy Spirit, it increased in numbers** (Acts 9:31).

**Scripture:** Acts 9:19-31
**Song:** "Great Is Thy Faithfulness"

A blog called "The Christian Pundit" recently noted a trend among young evangelicals: they're flocking to more traditional congregations that emphasize liturgy and church history. Blue jeans are out, and more formal church clothes are in. This seems to be reversing the trend of a generation ago, when 20-somethings opted to worship in a more casual, contemporary setting.

It can be hard to keep up with the trends. One minute hymns are out, and then, all of a sudden, everything old is new again. How should we reach others with the gospel? Should we focus on the musical style or vestments, or should we bring in the latest celebrity preachers?

Today's verse reminds us that the power of the Holy Spirit will grow the church, not our efforts alone. Our main focus should be on faithfully proclaiming the gospel and living in the fear of the Lord. Trends will come and go, but one thing never changes: the invitation to repent and receive forgiveness in Christ.

While God may call different congregations to reach different groups of people through different worship styles, we can never go wrong if we remain focused on the main thing: that God was in Christ reconciling the world to himself. Let that message be our theme as we seek to reach the world for Him.

**Gracious God,** thank You for Your faithfulness in building Your church. Purify me by Your Holy Spirit, so I can reach others for You. Through Christ, amen.

# Victory Redefined

**Can anything ever separate us from Christ's love? Does it mean he no longer loves us if we have trouble or calamity . . . ?** (Romans 8:35, *New Living Translation*).

**Scripture:** Romans 8:31-39
**Song:** "O the Deep, Deep Love of Jesus"

It didn't feel like a victory. The words to "O the Deep, Deep Love of Jesus" didn't arouse warm feelings when the soloist sang it. My daughter had committed suicide, and I was attending her memorial service. I stood at the starting point of a long, difficult journey of healing. I didn't feel comfort, love, victory, or hope—but I knew such things existed. That hope was the knot at the end of my rope, and I clung to the lifeline.

The next year tested the truth of my favorite Bible verse, "Can anything ever separate us from Christ's love?" (Romans 8:35, *NLT*). That is, do you still believe God loves you when you're in deep trouble? When you're poor and hungry? (I could have added: when your daughter commits suicide?)

Paul's conclusion confounds me: "Despite all these things, overwhelming victory is ours through Christ, who loved us" (v. 37, *NLT*) Despite evidence to the contrary, I do know God loves us. He promises not a victory won by the skin of our teeth, but an overwhelming victory. Such love wins through, even as hope lies shattered on the floor.

**Loving Father,** Your love is inscrutable, yet limitless. Teach me to trust it amidst the most trying times. Come with Your healing comfort, even now. Through Christ, amen.

October 12–18. **Darlene Franklin** lives in a retirement home in Purcell, Oklahoma. The author of 25 books, she continues to write full-time.

# The Son of God . . . for You?

**Then those who were in the boat came and worshiped Him, saying, "Truly You are the Son of God"** (Matthew 14:33, *New King James Version*).

**Scripture:** Matthew 14:22-33
**Song:** "You Are God Alone"

GODISNOWHERE. Our worship leader wrote those capital letters jumbled together on a blackboard and asked us what we saw. Despair or hope? God is *nowhere*, or God is *now here?*

That simple sermon has stayed with me more than any other Christmas message. For the first time, I understood why Christians put so much emphasis on Jesus' birth: He is Immanuel, God with us.

*God is now here!* God, all of God, the one who created the earth and stopped the Red Sea is with us. God is now here. He is also all man, all here, all of God bound up in a helpless infant.

That was my aha! moment when I worshipped: Truly this man is the Son of God, in my heart as well as my head.

Today's Scripture describes an aha moment for the apostles. Others—Jesus' family, demons—had called Jesus the Son of God. Before this time, the disciples had called him Master. What opened their eyes—Jesus walking on water? Saving Peter from drowning? Stopping the storm as soon as He climbed in the boat? And for that matter, what has made you say: "Jesus is the Son of God"?

**Lord,** You are God. I see You in the world You created. You reveal yourself in Your Word. And I know You in my heart. May I live each moment of my life with the confidence that You will help me walk on rough waters daily. In Jesus' name, amen.

# Something Greater Here

**I tell you that something greater than the temple is here. If you had known what these words mean, 'I desire mercy, not sacrifice,' you would not have condemned the innocent.** (Matthew 12:6, 7).

**Scripture:** Matthew 12:1-8
**Song:** "Sanctuary"

One year, my family made a whirlwind trip from Oklahoma to Ellis Island in a week. We drove past miles and miles of crops in the state of Illinois. To commemorate the occasion, we stopped and took a picture of our two preschoolers hiding in the cornstalks.

When I read about Jesus and His disciples walking through wheat fields, I remembered that day. Hungry and tired, the disciples didn't think about Sabbath rules. They saw a food source and took advantage of it. So the religious leaders pounced.

Something greater is at work here. Worship was never the sum of the law. Rather, the law pointed to deeper truths: Mercy, not sacrifice. People, not rules.

On our trip, we didn't make it to church. But we had many opportunities to worship. We saw the God who gave us food and carved caves into the mountains. We thanked Him for our country at the Statue of Liberty. He joined in our fellowship with friends. Worship doesn't depend on time and place. It depends on our hearts.

**Lord of the Sabbath,** You still desire mercy and not sacrifice. When my shortsighted heart focuses on unimportant details, correct my vision to see people as You see them. Then make me a conduit of Your mercy. In Jesus' name, amen.

# By No Means

**Peter said, "By no means, Lord, for I have never eaten any-thing unholy and unclean"** (Acts 10:14, *New American Standard Bible*).

**Scripture:** Acts 10:1-16
**Song:** "I Surrender All"

Due to a recent health crisis, I've moved from my house to a retirement home. In doing so, I had to downsize my belongings to what I most wanted to preserve. At the top of my list, right after the books I've written and my family pictures, were my Christmas ornaments. The collection tells my family's story, and I collected them based on many cherished memories.

Unfortunately, my collection came into conflict with my son's point of view about Christmas. He chooses to celebrate only the religious observances mentioned by name in the Bible, which shuts out the word *Christmas*. (This, of course, is clearly a minority opinion!) When he refused to keep my ornaments, I wasn't so much surprised as disappointed.

Did God feel the same when Peter said, "By no means, Lord"? Did the disciple hesitate before he uttered the words that contra-dicted each other? (If Jesus was his *Lord*, Peter shouldn't have said *no*.) Our arguments today may still hinge on food and holi-days. Or they might go on to differences in church ordinances or worship styles. In such gray matters, let us be careful not to say "by no means, Lord" when He says to "get up and eat."

**O God,** how many times have I called You "Lord" and yet have refused to obey? For-give me. Tame my pride when I have looked down on others who don't worship as I do. Let me never say no when You are urging me to say yes. In Jesus' name, amen.

# From Doubt to Certainty

**Arise therefore, go down and go with them, doubting nothing; for I have sent them** (Acts 10:20, *New King James Version*).

**Scripture:** Acts 10:17-23
**Song:** "O Hope of Every Contrite Heart"

Six-year-old Ruby Bridges performed one of the bravest acts in the history of the United States. She simply attended her first day of first grade in 1960, in New Orleans. She was the first and the only black student in this all-white school. In many ways, she symbolized the wave of school desegregation that was changing the landscape of American education.

The Bridges family attended church while they debated the wisdom of pitting their daughter against centuries of ingrained racial hatred. But when the government—dare we say God?—sent federal marshals, they allowed Ruby to go with them. Did they make the decision without reservations? I doubt it.

Peter stood at such a crossroads between faith and doubt. Was the message of salvation for the Jews only—or for all the people of the earth? But God said: "Go with them. Don't doubt."

A risky faith acts in spite of doubt. I may doubt that I will succeed. I may doubt my own strength. But I place my hope in the God who gives me everything I need and who makes me strong.

A new school—a new church—a new job. Wherever God leads, we can move forward with Him in confidence.

**Almighty and everlasting God,** sometimes You lead me to do things that frighten me. Shine Your light on my path, that I may follow You step by step, day by day. May I discern the difference between dreams sent by You and my own selfish desires. In Jesus' name I pray. Amen.

# Eyes to See

**God raised Him up on the third day and granted that He become visible, not to all the people, but to witnesses who were chosen beforehand by God** (Acts 10:40, 41, *New American Standard Bible*).

**Scripture:** Acts 10:39-48
**Song:** "Open My Eyes"

When my family went traveling, three of us kids crowded into the back seat. As the trip stretched to long hours eating up the highway between Kentucky and Wisconsin, we played games. One involved spotting letters in alphabetical order. Some were easy to find. Others, like a *Q* or a *Z*, rarely showed up on billboard signs. That's when we scouted license plates.

Sometimes my brother found a letter that I missed. When I claimed I saw it, my dad told me, "No, you didn't." I pouted. I had no chance to win if I had to wait for the next time a *Q* showed up on a road sign.

I had missed letters hidden in plain sight. Something similar to that happened at Jesus' resurrection. Not everyone saw Him. The soldiers guarding the tomb? They slept through the most momentous event of their lives. The priests? By the time they were called to the tomb, Jesus had gone.

God handpicked the witnesses to Jesus's resurrection. He became visible when He chose—without benefit of special effects. Even so today God has given us eyes to see, eyes of faith, a heart-vision granted to us from Heaven.

**Light of the World,** as those disciples of old told the story of Jesus' resurrection, let me also bear witness to what I have seen and heard. Through Christ, amen.

# Guess Who Moved?

**Now we are all here in the presence of God to listen to everything the Lord has commanded you to tell us** (Acts 10:33).

**Scripture:** Acts 10:24-38
**Song:** "In the Garden"

"Eighty percent of success is showing up," said Woody Allen. Every month, I receive a calendar of daily activities at the home where I live. All I have to do is show up to have popcorn and a movie, get my hair cut, or sing hymns with a visiting church.

Excuses abound for not attending, though. I might not receive help in time. My therapist arrives to work with me. I forget.

Most disappointing, sometimes the people who promise to come . . . *don't!* That happened last Sunday when the local church group didn't show up. Their pianist was unavailable. Even worse, some weeks I just choose to remain in my room. What would the church be like today if Cornelius hadn't sent for Peter, or if Peter had refused to go?

When we do gather together, God descends on that lonely lobby. We sing the familiar hymns of our childhood. Unable to sing, I cry at God's beauty.

Even when alone, God invites me to come into His presence, be it by reading the Bible on the computer, by singing hymns and praise songs, or by silent prayer. God meets me there.

I cannot hear what God has to say if I don't take the time to listen. As someone has said, "If you feel far from God, guess who moved?"

**God,** You invite me to worship, whether on my own or with others, in the silence of nature or in the symphony of music. When You call, may I respond. In Christ, amen.

# Default to God

**I will also make you a light for the Gentiles, that my salvation may reach to the ends of the earth** (Isaiah 49:6).

**Scripture:** Isaiah 49:5-7
**Song:** "Make Me a Servant"

At the end of our horse pasture, there's an old cedar tree whose branches formed perfect junctures for a tree house. With our kids, we spent an afternoon rounding up old boards from the barn, a discarded telephone cable reel, rope, and nails.

We measured and sawed the boards to make a square frame that would fit between the branches. We disassembled the cable reel, converting it into a floor to wedge within our framework. Using a ladder and rope, we hoisted the foundation pieces upward, then nailed everything together in the crooks of the tree.

Our tree house hosted many adventures, and even served as a hideout. Little Marci found refuge there when she ran away from home with a jelly sandwich, a copy of *Little House on the Prairie*, and her stuffed rabbit. Now, 20 years later, our little tree house, with steps nailed into the trunk and rope to swing out with, still serves as a treasured setting for pursuing God's heart.

Isaiah poised himself to seek God. He listened as the Lord shared His vision for his life. God designed Isaiah to be a servant and commissioned him as a catalyst for restoration.

**Dear Father in Heaven,** I'm grateful for Your purposeful design—from houses to hearts. In any creative endeavor, may I look to You for the meaning and purpose to infuse it. In Jesus' name I pray. Amen.

October 19–25. **Vicki L. Hodges** lives in the mountains of western Colorado with her family. She's a high school Spanish teacher who loves to travel.

# A Grooved Heart

**Whoever drinks the water I give them will never thirst. Indeed, the water I give them will become in them a spring of water welling up to eternal life** (John 4:14).

**Scripture:** John 4:3-14
**Song:** "Springs of Living Water"

In today's verses, we meet a Samaritan woman who encountered the Lord at Jacob's well. After an intensely personal conversation, He talked with the woman about living water and eternal life. She was forever changed.

Hand-dug wells in ancient Israel were deep, sometimes with depths of 60 to over 100 feet, depending on the water table level. People fastened a bucket or clay jar to a rope and lowered it into the well, allowed the container to fill, then heaved it up. Over time, friction from the rope's sliding carved deep grooves into the well's "curbs," its top edges.

When I was in college, I was involved with a campus ministry whose director, Ron, was a man of great spiritual stature. He so enjoyed encouraging believers in their spiritual growth and relished helping them become disciple-makers.

Because of Ron's passion for people and God's Word, in a process of disciple-multiplication, countless people around the world are now walking with Jesus. The curbs of Ron's heart contain deep grooves from constantly drawing the living water of God's Word and sharing its truths of eternal life.

**Lord,** I'm thirsting for You. Would You fill me with a conscious awareness of Your presence and with a passion for Your living Word? Please wear a groove in my heart as I draw in Your life-giving water. In Jesus' name, amen.

# Prepared, Not Frightened

**In your hearts revere Christ as Lord. Always be prepared to give an answer to everyone who asks you to give the reason for the hope that you have** (1 Peter 3:15).

**Scripture:** 1 Peter 3:13-18
**Song:** "The Battle Belongs to the Lord"

Our dream vacation to Sitka, Alaska, quickly approached, and we discussed itinerary options with Mark and Hedy. Hedy, proud of her Alaskan native heritage, wanted us to visit her parents and experience her rich Tlingit culture. When she suggested hiking, she casually referenced the abundance of sporting goods stores that sold pepper spray.

Steve and I exchanged glances. "Hedy, why did you mention pepper spray?"

"Well, it would only be necessary if bears attack us."

Bears! What would we do? flee? scream? spray ourselves with pepper? Hedy informed us that young school children receive extensive training for living in bear country. Adequate education, preparation, and a tranquil spirit are essential.

Perhaps one of our greatest privileges is sharing our faith with others. During any given conversation, such an opportunity may arise. Sometimes I am prepared to share and do so with confidence. Other times, my instinct is to flee. I lose my nerve and forget that God has empowered me. In His strength I can speak of Him with grace, love, and all humility. (Preparation and a tranquil spirit are essential.)

**Father,** thank You for the reliable, relevant truths in Your Word. The hope of the gospel is the encouraging message I want to share. In Jesus' name, amen.

# Fire and Rain

**His purpose was to create in himself one new humanity out of the two, thus making peace** (Ephesians 2:15).

**Scripture:** Ephesians 2:11-22
**Song:** "My Faith Has Found a Resting Place"

"The fire stopped 500 yards from my apartment." Aimee's words flooded us with peace. Our daughter had evacuated twice from the 2012 Waldo Canyon fire in Colorado Springs. Tearfully, from her front porch, Amy viewed once lovely homes now standing as smoking hulks, with blackened vegetation replacing verdant wildlife habitats.

"I'm in the middle of a flash flood warning!" A year later, Aimee's words blazed through the phone. She had received numerous calls urging her to be prepared to move to higher ground. Midsummer cloudbursts assaulted the charred, eroded terrain. Forests no longer restrained rushing water. Once again, the elements were at odds with humanity, potential enemies of the land, poised to cause devastation.

Despite reseeding efforts and the installation of massive drainage systems, threats still existed. Similarly, Paul declared that many live as enemies of the cross of Christ—and their potential destiny is devastating. But for followers of Jesus, our citizenship is in Heaven. We are part of an eternal reclamation project!

Thank you, **Lord,** for Your sacrifice on the cross. Because of Your shed blood, I have forgiveness and am no longer an enemy, but a member of Your family. Thank You for the peace that passes understanding. I'm grateful You are transforming me into the likeness of Christ. In Your holy name I pray. Amen.

# The Please Car

**Join together in following my example, brothers and sisters, and just as you have us as a model, keep your eyes on those who live as we do** (Philippians 3:17).

**Scripture:** Philippians 3:17-21
**Song:** "There Is a Redeemer"

"Imitation is not just the sincerest form of flattery, it's the sincerest form of learning." The second half of George Shaw's statement appears to agree with the apostle Paul's advice in today's passage. Paul modeled a reproducible lifestyle because the one he followed was Jesus Christ, who lived a perfect life.

Mark and Hedy are teaching modes of transportation to 20-month-old Jason. They tell him about a vehicle's name and offer some accompanying representation of it. So, when he sees a type of vehicle, he names it and makes an association.

Recently, Mark displayed a picture of a fire truck, and Jason muttered something vaguely resembling "fire," and then blurted, "Truck! VROOM!" While chasing Daddy in the front yard, a jet flew over, and Jason screeched to a halt. Pointing to the sky he said, "Plane! Fly!" He was definitely learning to imitate his parents' examples. Later that evening, I showed him a picture of a police car, and he rubbed his chest in a circle with a flat palm (sign language for "please"), voiced "Car," and made sounds like a siren! Like followers of Jesus, sometimes Jason can produce an accurate imitation, and other times, he's derailed.

**Jesus,** thank You for keeping all the commandments perfectly on my behalf—and for offering the perfect sacrifice for my sin. Now help me live for You by following in Your footsteps. Praise Your holy name. Amen.

# The Band-Aid® Box

**When he arrived and saw what the grace of God had done, he was glad and encouraged them all to remain true to the Lord with all their hearts** (Acts 11:23).

**Scripture:** Acts 11:19-26
**Song:** "He Ransomed Me"

"What's so special about a Band-Aid® box?" When Steve's dad initially showed him the container, Steve didn't comprehend its importance. The rusty metal box, tied to a fence post, stood at the end of their graveled county road. His dad opened the tin, revealing a crumpled paper containing neighbors' names.

Each neighbor owned shares of irrigation water and notified the ditch company when they intended to utilize it. They received permission to divert water into their ditches on requested dates. The "ditch rider" added their names to the box.

Seven years ago, Steve and I assumed the responsibility for irrigating Dad's property. After our attempt at ordering water, we sprinted out, eager to route the first gushes. We encountered a dry channel. "Where's our water?"

Our parched ditch still thirsted at 8:00 a.m. so we drove to the Band-Aid® box. The document lacked our name! Steve contacted the ditch rider about our negative water flow.

When early believers shared the gospel of Jesus Christ, mercy met grace. Many added their names to the registry of those who draw living water.

**Lord,** even at my best, I'm unworthy. I'm thankful for Your sacrificial death and resurrection so I could have citizenship in Heaven. Please write my name in the Lamb's book of life for all of eternity. In Jesus' name, amen.

# Head Toward That Rock!

**The Spirit told me to have no hesitation about going with them** (Acts 11:12).

**Scripture:** Acts 11:1-18
**Song:** "Be Thou My Vision"

*Goal!* Celebrating another beach soccer victory, our teenaged students plunged into the ocean, splashing near the shoreline. Without warning, a flash rip current seized Andrew and Tyler, dragging them out to sea. Chaperones ordered everyone back to land, then scaled a nearby boulder. Andrew swam parallel with the beach, escaping the grip of the rip.

Whitecaps volleyed Tyler from boulder to boulder, adjacent to the headland. Luigi shouted, "Relax!" while Tyler wrestled for his life. As waves dragged Tyler around the corner of the cliffs, concealing him from sight, he hollered, "I can't keep swimming!" We prayed.

Suddenly, Tyler reappeared. Luigi bellowed, *"Head toward that rock!"* Tyler paddled forward and, finally, crawling onto the rock, gripping securely, he embraced safety. Seconds later, the sea scraped him off, plunging him under. When he surfaced, powerful waves blasted him near Luigi, now close enough to toss a boogie board. Tyler clutched it while Luigi hauled him in.

Peter listened carefully to ensure He heard God correctly. Then, convinced of God's instructions, he proceeded without hesitation. That is always the way to service . . . and safety.

**Lord,** when You show me what to do, I want to respond immediately. Give me a heart that listens to You and a willingness to act without hesitation. Remove any excuses I allow to stand in the way of Your will. In Jesus' name, amen.

# Delivered from Death

**In my distress I called to the LORD; I cried to my God for help. From his temple he heard my voice; my cry came before him, into his ears** (Psalm 18:6).

**Scripture:** Psalm 18:1-9
**Song:** "A Mighty Fortress Is Our God"

Talk about rip currents! Here's another item: A 12-year-old boy struggled in potentially deadly tide waters. Nicole, also 12 years of age, turned her boogie board toward the deeper water and headed out to help. She reached Dale and got him onto her board. As they headed in, a fierce wave knocked them off the board, and other rescuers had to wade in to help pull Dale out. But without Nicole's initial efforts, it is doubtful Dale would have been saved.

How grateful would you be to someone who saved your life? Psalmist David expresses his gratitude to God for repeated moments of deliverance. In vivid terms, he describes what one might express today as "my life flashing before my eyes."

I love the way David connects his prayer to God's response. The Lord is roused . . . and rises to the rescue.

Were it not David we might think the writer is a bit conceited. How can he be so sure that God, in His temple, hears his prayer? But this is the God that all of His children serve. He hears our prayer and rises to rescue us in all our times of need.

**Lord,** I'm not in such distress and danger as David faced. But I thank You that even if my life were threatened, I could count on You to be there with me. In Christ, amen.

October 26–31. **Dan Nicksich** and his wife, Donna, live in Grant, Michigan, where Dan is senior minister of the Northland Church of Christ.

# Seek and Go

**Let your hand rest on the man at your right hand, the son of man you have raised up for yourself** (Psalm 80:17).

**Scripture:** Psalm 80:1-3, 7, 17-19
**Song:** "All Hail the Power of Jesus' Name"

Holly was in tears. She and her boyfriend had fallen to temptation. Her family's negative feelings toward this relationship intensified, and Holly had left home for a long time. Now she sought reconciliation with God and her parents.

Israel, represented by Ephraim, Benjamin, and Manasseh sought reconciliation with God. In a surprising twist, the Psalm writer turns the focus of restoration to the "man at [God's] right hand, the son of man" in fact.

Whether it's to ancient Israel or to us today, God's offer of reconciliation comes through this same Son of man, the one seated at His right hand. The New Testament is clear: this man is Jesus, the only means of peace between sinful humanity and a holy God. There's no other possibility for reconciliation.

Holly's willingness to confess her sin, coupled with her tears of regret, suggest a level of repentance that touches the heart of God. What remains to be seen: Will her parents welcome home a prodigal daughter?

Is there anyone in the church with whom you are at odds these days? Seek the reconciliation that only Christ can bring. Go to your brother, your sister, without delay.

**Heavenly Father,** how difficult it can be to forgive those who sin against us. How difficult to forgive those who defy us. It helps me, even more, to appreciate the depth and breadth of Your forgiveness toward me. Thank You, in Jesus' name. Amen.

# Grab My Hand!

**At the first light of dawn, the king got up and hurried to the lions' den** (Daniel 6:19).

**Scripture:** Daniel 6:19-24
**Song:** "Leaning on the Everlasting Arms"

Dan's wife and daughter were about to head out in their kayaks when Dan noticed a man in the water nearby. He was struggling to stay afloat while two frightened children clung to him. Dan edged out into the water and extended his hand. He was about to slip into a hole when he heard a voice behind him, "Grab my hand." Together they pulled the three to safety—and soon Dan waved goodbye to his wife and daughter as they paddled downstream. Later that evening, Dan commented on his daughter's strength. "But Dan," his wife said, "Sue was already in her kayak alongside of me."

"Well, who was it that grabbed my hand?" Dan asked.

"There was no one there; it looked as if you reached back to balance yourself and, next thing we saw, you were pulling them in." Had Dan been helped by an angel, a ministering spirit?

We know the biblical Daniel was helped that way! Though some seem to doubt the presence of angels, or even the possibility of miracles, I'm thankful an ancient king ventured out to check on Daniel in the morning. Daniel didn't give up hope.

While we may not deliberately seek miracles or feel we must put God to the test, both Dan and Daniel can affirm: our God ministers to us through myriad ways.

**Lord,** I thank You that You have various ways to express Your omnipotent power and matchless goodness to us. Through Christ, amen.

# Inspiring the King

I issue a decree that in every part of my kingdom people must fear and reverence the God of Daniel. "For he is the living God and he endures forever; his kingdom will not be destroyed, his dominion will never end" (Daniel 6:26).

**Scripture:** Daniel 6:25-28
**Song:** "Dare to Be a Daniel"

Jerry pedals his bike all over town delivering newspapers. To his customers, it seems as if he's been doing it forever. In fact, he started when he was 10 and will soon be 40. Jerry, you see, is someone we call "special needs." But his customers love him. You can always count on Jerry getting your paper to you. You can also count on his smiling face and a friendly greeting.

"What makes you so happy, Jerry?" one of his customers asked. Jerry answered without hesitation. "Jesus. He saved me, and someday I won't be like this anymore. I'll be just like everyone else when I'm up in Heaven with Him."

When his church was preparing for Friend Day, Jerry handed out invitations to any customer he happened to see. Several came to church that Sunday. "We're here because of Jerry," they said. But many still wonder if Jerry understands just how powerful his example has proved to be.

I may not inspire a king like Daniel inspired King Darius. I may not be delivered miraculously. But, like Jerry, I hope there are others who are moved to praise God because of me.

**Lord,** I am humbled by those like Jerry whose simple faith and trusting obedience bear such awesome fruit. As I learn from their example, I pray You will use me in similar fashion. In Jesus' name I pray. Amen.

# I Told You So!

**Do not be afraid, Paul. You must stand trial before Caesar; and God has graciously given you the lives of all who sail with you** (Acts 27:23, 24).

**Scripture:** Acts 27:14-25
**Song:** "Soon and Very Soon"

Few things are as irritating as someone who likes to say, "I told you so." Perhaps it's different if the speaker is an inspired apostle of the Lord. For example, Paul had every right to say, "I told you so." He had offered advice against the timing of a ship's voyage. Now battered by an unrelenting storm, Paul addresses the fearful crew and passengers.

He didn't stop with, "I told you so," and I marvel at his calm, deliberate speech. After all, these are sailors he's talking to! Yet to a boatload of salty seafarers, hardened Roman soldiers, and other prisoners, Paul says there's no reason to worry. Why? Because an angel told him so! Would you be so quick to tell such a crowd about personal angelic visits? Paul didn't hesitate.

Apparently something about Paul inspired trust and serenity. Few men could speak as convincingly in such distressing circumstances but Paul pulled it off.

If you're going to say, "I told you so," think twice. Do you have words of assurance to follow up with? Do you have a solution to the problem, the issue being faced? If not, silence might be the preferred response.

**Lord,** I want to be the one lifting up prayer in distressing times, the one others look to for words of calm assurance. And may I always think twice when tempted to say, "I told you so." In the name of Jesus, amen.

# Trust His Answers?

**"You're out of your mind," they told her. When she kept insisting that it was so, they said, "It must be his angel"** (Acts 12:15).

**Scripture:** Acts 12:12-18
**Song:** "Lord, Listen to Your Children Praying"

Martin always seems to struggle financially. His latest trial involved a car that would prove too costly to fix. "I'm praying for a new car," he said. "But money's very tight right now."

The next day Martin was unexpectedly called to work overtime. Then, he was surprised by a check in the mail for over $700. It was for excess escrow funds withheld by his credit union. "I knew God was going to provide. I just didn't know it would be this quickly." I've heard story after story like this. We pray for help yet are surprised when God provides it.

The church was praying for Peter. He was imprisoned by King Herod, who had recently killed James, his fellow apostle. But when angels release Peter, the servant girl is so excited at Peter's arrival that she forgets to unlock the door. The prayer meeting can't believe what they're hearing.

"What's that? Peter's at the door? It can't be; he's in prison!"

I wonder if any of them ever caught the irony of their belief-inspired prayer for Peter . . . coupled with their statement of disbelief when their prayer was answered?

I wonder how faithfully we are praying? Wouldn't it be great if, after praying, we simply trusted His answers?

**Lord,** thank You for hearing my prayers. My desire is simply to be a person of faith, always trusting as I await Your answer. In Jesus' name, amen.

# DEVOTIONS®

## NOVEMBER

Giving joyful thanks to the Father, . . . he has
rescued us . . . and brought us into the kingdom.

—*Colossians 1:12, 13*

**Gary Wilde,** Editor      **Margaret Williams,** Project Editor      Photo iStock | Thinkstock®

*DEVOTIONS®* is published quarterly by Standard Publishing, Cincinnati, Ohio, www.standardpub.com.
© 2014 by Standard Publishing. All rights reserved. Topics based on the Home Daily Bible Readings,
International Sunday School Lessons. © 2012 by the Committee on the Uniform Series. Printed in
the U.S.A. All Scripture quotations, unless otherwise indicated, are taken from the HOLY BIBLE,
*NEW INTERNATIONAL VERSION®. NIV®.* Copyright © 1973, 1978, 1984, 2011 by Biblica, Inc.®
Used by permission of Zondervan. All rights reserved worldwide. *New American Standard Bible®,*
(*NASB*) Copyright © 1960, 1962, 1963, 1968, 1971, 1972, 1973, 1975, 1977, 1995 by The Lock-
man Foundation. Used by permission. (www.Lockman.org). *Holy Bible, New Living Translation*
(*NLT*), © 1996, 2004, 2007. Tyndale House Publishers. Scripture quotations marked (*NKJV*) are
taken from the *New King James Version®.* Copyright © 1982 by Thomas Nelson, Inc. Used by
permission. All rights reserved. *King James Version* (*KJV*), public domain.

# Delivered!

**Peter followed him out of the prison, but he had no idea that what the angel was doing was really happening; he thought he was seeing a vision** (Acts 12:9).

**Scripture:** Acts 12:1-11
**Song:** "Faith Is the Victory"

In July of 2002, nine Pennsylvania coal miners were rescued after being trapped underground for more than three days. Some hailed it as a miracle after a team successfully drilled a rescue shaft down to the men. As the miners emerged, one by one in the rescue capsule most seemed dazed as if in disbelief.

Peter's rescue reads the same way. Released by an angel, he struggles with the reality of his escape. He thinks it's all a dream or a vision. King Herod had already killed James, a fellow apostle; surely Herod would kill him next.

We won't always know why some are rescued and some are not. There's no explaining why some are delivered and some are not. Miracles aren't always the order of the day; some continue to suffer at the hands of evil men.

It would seem that the best course is always to center ourselves in God's will. If rescues and miracles come our way, we accept them as opportunities to continue serving. If suffering is the order of the day, our faithfulness continues to point the way to Jesus.

**Lord**, Your will. Nothing more, nothing else, nothing less. Help me to see every situation that arises in the light of Your will for my life. In Jesus' name, amen.

November 1. **Dan Nicksich** and his wife, Donna, live in Grant, Michigan, where Dan is senior minister of the Northland Church of Christ.

# Being There for One Another

**I long to see you so that I may impart to you some spiritual gift to make you strong—that is, that you and I may be mutually encouraged by each other's faith** (Romans 1:11, 12).

**Scripture:** Romans 1:8-15
**Song:** "The Bond of Love"

"Why did you let go of my hand?" Sitting in her living room only hours after her husband's death, I held her hand through the whole visit. But as soon as I let go, she wanted to feel that personal warmth again. The words, the laughter, the memories, and the tears flowed freely. But those things could have happened over the phone. She needed a comforting friend holding her hand, physically present in her grief.

We need the personal presence of people we love and people who love us. Four times in today's passage Paul explains to the Roman Christians how deeply he longs to be with them. Messengers were adequate. Letters were necessary. Hearsay was enlightening. But being in Rome with them would make encouragement and ministry to them more practical. So he prayed fervently for the opportunity.

That's why hospitals and military units have chaplains. It's why we wash feet and lay on hands to pray. The physical presence of other believers delivers tangible support, encouragement, and comfort to those who need it.

**Emmanuel**, give me the awareness to see those around me who need my physical presence. Then give me the grace to show up. Through Christ, amen.

November 2–8. **Matthew Boardwell** is an avid nonfiction reader and enthusiastic musician. He is husband to Pam, father of nine, and a church-planting missionary in the west of Ireland.

# A Dose of Reality

**You are a God of forgiveness, gracious and compassionate, slow to anger and abounding in lovingkindness; and You did not forsake them** (Nehemiah 9:17, *New American Standard Bible*).

**Scripture:** Nehemiah 9:6-21
**Song:** "Come, Ye Sinners, Poor and Needy"

When I was a child, I used to sit upside-down on the sofa and imagine that the ceiling was the floor. In that world, I would have to step over door frames and around light fixtures. I would reach up to set out plates on the underside of the table. Sometimes I'd imagine that kids were in charge, too. Then parents would have to obey and do the chores; kids could just have fun. In other words, I imagined things were the opposite of reality.

What if God were the opposite of reality? What if He weren't a forgiving God, full of grace and kindness? What if He were quick to anger and meager in love?

Certainly, that sort of God would have abandoned Israel in the desert. After all their rebellion and obstinacy, He would have washed His hands of them. He would have let them hunger, thirst, and perish. In fact, He might have abandoned them to slavery in the first place.

Wouldn't He have done the same with us in that topsy-turvy, imaginary spiritual landscape? Instead, He loves and forgives us, shows us patience and grace, and calls us His treasured children. Sometimes, it takes a prayer of confession to remember it.

**Father**, I'm humbled when I remember who You really are. Forgive me for projecting onto You my own inconsistent love. Today I gratefully receive Your grace and kindness. It covers my sin and nudges me to righteousness. In Christ, amen.

# Solving the Mystery

**Now to Him who is able to establish you according to my gospel and the preaching of Jesus Christ, according to the revelation of the mystery which has been kept secret for long ages past but now is manifested** (Romans 16:25, 26, *New American Standard Bible*).

**Scripture:** Romans 16:25-27
**Song:** "O Come, O Come, Emmanuel"

Don't you love a good mystery film? There's the challenge of figuring out the puzzle. There's the tension of suspense. There are all the clues, obvious and obscure. And of course, there's the satisfying conclusion when all the clues come suddenly together.

Paul writes that his good news was the ultimate in mysteries, a secret kept hidden and finally revealed in Jesus Christ. In fact, for generations there were clues. Prophecies pointed to a certain kind of messiah, coming from a specific place, doing a particular work. According to these clues, God would personally come to the rescue. The Savior would live and die not only for His own nation, but for the Gentiles as well. Then everyone could be aware of the secret plans of God to save the whole world.

Throughout his letter, the apostle revealed how these pieces fit together. Overjoyed, he concluded with ecstatic praise to the God who designed and carried out such a magnificent plan. And we—if we could identify with those first Christian hearers, we too would marvel at and proclaim the revealed wisdom of God.

**Eternal God,** You could have left us in the dark, surrounded by questions. But You are the God who reveals himself. One step at a time You have shown Your plan to the world. And by Your mercy, You revealed yourself to me too. Through Christ, amen.

# Coming Out of Hiding

**Nothing in all creation is hidden from God's sight. Everything is uncovered and laid bare before the eyes of him to whom we must give account** (Hebrews 4:13).

**Scripture:** Hebrews 4:12-16
**Song:** "Search Me, O God"

Joe has an unusual pain in his side. It's never bothered him before, but it's pretty intense these days. He figures it will go away, but when it doesn't he still won't see a doctor. You see, he doesn't want to know for sure whether something is wrong (even though he knows for sure that something is wrong). So he puts up with pain. He puts off the tests. When it can no longer be avoided, Joe will find out what he has suspected all along. He has a serious cancer . . . that's no longer treatable.

Ever since Adam and Eve covered themselves with fig leaves to escape the piercing gaze of God, human beings have specialized in covering up their sin. Hebrews tells us how useless these efforts are. The razor of God's Word slices right through our evasions, getting to the heart. Every effort to obscure or deflect God's notice proves futile. There is nothing He cannot see and eventually, we must face Him.

The cure for our sin is the mercy and grace of a sympathetic Savior. Jesus has all the mercy we need. But first we must submit ourselves to His soul-deep examination. Exposure is the way to healing.

**Gentle Healer,** I humbly offer my heart to You with all its broken pieces and dark sin stains. Apply Your grace and forgiveness to each flaw. Remake me in the image of Jesus. I know that He understands where I am. In Christ I pray. Amen.

# God Wants to Be with Us

**Look! God's dwelling place is now among the people, and he will dwell with them** (Revelation 21:3).

**Scripture:** Revelation 21:1-5
**Song:** "The Kingdom of God"

Many people believe that if there is a God, He is indifferent to us. All they need to do is read the first and last chapters of the Bible to see how laughable that is!

God wanted a walk *together*. He wanted human fellowship. He offered humans His tangible presence and personal interaction. The only thing that impeded Adam and Eve being with Him was their own shame. Still, even their shame didn't keep God from pursuing them or addressing their need. Even in their sin, He wanted them. He still sought and found them. He still provided for them and promised a rescue.

One day, He will build His children a new Heaven and a new earth. He will scrape off the old and lay down the new. He will wipe every tear away and banish death and pain. He's moving history toward that final chapter. It's what He's always wanted.

He still offers His permanent presence. His tangible lasting friendship is there for all who will receive it. He is preparing a future set free from heartache. When we arrive, we will discover that His longing has always been what we've wanted most. Belonging with Him—being home.

**Father**, what a joy it will be when I am finally gathered home where I belong. With the rest of Your children I look forward to a sin-free, sorrow-free, sickness-free future with You. As much as I long for that, it is a thrill to know that You want it even more. I praise You, through the precious name of Jesus. Amen.

# Welcomed In

**He redeemed us in order that the blessing given to Abraham might come to the Gentiles through Christ Jesus** (Galatians 3:14).

**Scripture:** Galatians 3:6-14
**Song:** "Room at the Cross for You"

Have you ever been left out? The third wheel in a friendship? The new kid who can't find his way into a clique? An outsider painfully aware of how much she doesn't belong?

What does it take to belong? You can crash your way into the circle. Sometimes that works, but most of the time the circle becomes more irritated than welcoming. What works better is for someone in that friendship to reach out to you—and the more important the person, the better the reception of the others.

During Jesus' earthly ministry, many assumed that the kingdom of God was just another way to describe Israel. Sure, a non-Jew could convert, but very few would ever bother. So the circle was small, as small as a small nation. It would take divine intervention to invite the rest of the world in.

One of the two in this relationship between God and Israel reached out to us. The most important one took the initiative to bring us in. He reached out to us, Jew or Gentile, who were excluded. He died for the sin of everyone, Jew or Gentile. With no other sacrifices or ceremonies needed, He made us all children of Abraham.

**Lord,** You welcome the stranger and outcast. You welcomed me. Where would I be without Your love? For taking the initiative to find me and invite me in, I worship You. Grant me a love that welcomes others who are alienated too. In Jesus' name, amen.

# Too Heavy for Our Brothers

**Why do you try to test God by putting on the necks of Gentiles a yoke that neither we nor our ancestors have been able to bear?** (Acts 15:10).

**Scripture:** Acts 15:1-12
**Song:** "Jesus Paid It All"

When we go grocery shopping for our family of 11, we usually fill a car. When it's time to unload, the kids come out to help. Our 4-year-old can carry a couple loaves of bread. The older teens can carry a few gallons of milk. I can usually manage a half-dozen sacks on my own. But no one can carry the whole load alone. To try (or expect someone to try) is foolishness.

Maybe that's how Peter felt when some early Jewish Christians wanted new Gentile Christians to obey the law of Moses. The Gentiles could come in, but they'd have to comply.

This approach troubled Peter because he knew the Jewish experience personally. Once in a while, someone could get it right. They could follow the law, keep the feasts, maintain ritual purity, and do it all with a good heart . . . for a while. Before long, though, they would stumble into sin. The law was just too heavy for even the strongest to carry.

Peter also knew Jesus personally. He watched Him live. He heard His teaching. He remembered His death. He experienced Him alive. And he knew the law was no match for the freedom of salvation by grace through Him.

**Dear Lord,** thank You for lifting my heavy load for me. I never could have been disciplined or faithful enough to measure up to the law's exacting standard. So You measured up for me. Thanks be to You, through Your holy name. Amen.

# Danger Ahead, Turn Back

**Perhaps they will listen and each will turn from their evil ways. Then I will relent** (Jeremiah 26:3).

**Scripture:** Jeremiah 26:1-6
**Song:** "Turn Your Eyes upon Jesus"

The man stood in the fork of the highway. He wore a khaki shirt rolled up at the sleeves and a pair of faded blue jeans. He carried a shovel, which he was waving to get our attention. Although he wasn't wearing his uniform, my father recognized him as a U.S. Forest Ranger. Rangers working a fire line or other forest-related emergencies seldom dressed in their traditional hats or uniforms. Dad immediately brought our Chevy Suburban to a stop.

The officer told us we needed to turn around and go back the way we came. The river had washed out the road to the campground, and if we continued, the rocks and potholes would damage our vehicle. With his message delivered, he rushed back to warn two more approaching cars. They ignored him and continued down the road. He just shook his head in disbelief.

Likewise, Jeremiah tried to warn the people of Judah about their current path. By not listening to God or heeding His messengers, Judah was heading toward a judgment they would bring upon themselves. Our God has the same message of concern for the people our generation.

**God,** I want to walk only the pathway of Your will. However, if I am heading the wrong way, please stop me and point me in the right direction. In Jesus' name, amen.

November 9–15. **Charles Earl Harrel** was in church ministry for more than 30 years before stepping aside to pursue writing. He enjoys photography and playing the 12-string guitar.

# Unsearchable Treasure

**Unto me, who am less than the least of all saints, is this grace given, that I should preach among the Gentiles the unsearchable riches of Christ** (Ephesians 3:8, *King James Version*).

**Scripture:** Ephesians 3:7-12
**Song:** "My Precious Bible"

In 1847, John Sutter, a former artillery captain in the Swiss army, collaborated with James Marshall, a skilled carpenter, to build a sawmill along the South Fork of the American River in California. The mill, however, had a design flaw: the ditch that drained water from the waterwheel was too shallow.

It wasn't until Mr. Marshall decided, in January of 1848, to let the rushing current cut the mill's channel deeper that he discovered something entirely unexpected: gold.

"Unsearchable" normally means unreachable or beyond comprehension. However, some treasures only *appear* unsearchable—not because they're unreachable—but simply because we must dig deeper to find them. Such is the case with the unsearchable riches of Christ. The apostle Paul realized these boundless truths were searchable, after all. In fact, he not only preached them, he wrote about them in his epistles.

As you read the Scriptures each day, allow the Spirit of God to flow over your soul like living waters, opening a deep channel in your heart. Let Him wash away the familiar and uncover the unexpected. The Holy Spirit, who is our divine teacher, wants to reveal the richness and the depth of Christ's love.

**Precious Lord,** please open the treasure house of Your presence and draw me closer. Let me uncover all the riches hidden in Your Son. In Jesus' holy name, amen.

# First, Remove the Stone

**I will give you a new heart and put a new spirit within you; I will take the heart of stone out of your flesh and give you a heart of flesh** (Ezekiel 36:26, *New King James Version*).

**Scripture:** Ezekiel 36:22-30
**Song:** "Change My Heart, O God"

Daisy Lane was a great place for children to play. Our private street had endless potholes, a huge rock in the middle of the road, and plenty of untrimmed bushes to hide behind. It was also one of the last dirt roads in the city of La Cañada.

After years of costly repairs for their washed-out road, the residents of Daisy Lane, which included my family, decided to pave the old road. Everything went according to plan until the paving company tried to remove the rock. It wouldn't budge. They tried chipping away at it with a pick and a sledgehammer. Both tools bounced off. Even with a jackhammer, the rock remained intact. Finally, the supervisor called in a large bulldozer and backhoe. After hours of digging and pushing, the stone released its hold on the old road—and the paving began.

Before God can put a new spirit within us, He must remove the heart of stone in our lives. Spiritually speaking, a stony heart is a hindrance that makes us unteachable. Once removed, a heart of flesh, one that's responsive, sensitive, and compassionate, can be implanted. Such excavations are a specialty of the Holy Spirit. Just ask Him to renew a right spirit within you.

Mold me, **Lord,** into the servant You want me to be. If my heart has become hardened, then take out anything that hinders my Christian walk, give me a heart of compassion, and refresh my parched spirit. In Jesus' name, amen.

# Are You Willing?

**"Teacher, I will follow you wherever you go"** (Matthew 8:19).

**Scripture:** Matthew 8:18-22
**Song:** "I'll Go Where You Want Me to Go"

For two months I had been attending a little church in the farming town of Reedley, California. It was the last night of their 1972 missionary convention. My wife and I sat in the back row next to the center aisle. I don't recall the missionary's name or the country where she served. The "call," though, I remember in vivid detail.

After the speaker finished her talk, she asked everyone to bow their heads and close their eyes. Then came the first of two questions: "How many here tonight are willing to follow the Lord into the harvest field?" Being curious, I peered through half-closed eyelids. Most of the people raised their hands. Next, she asked, "But how many are willing to go wherever He calls you . . . or, if necessary, stay, wherever He wants you to stay?" Still peeking, I saw many of those hands lowered.

After the closing prayer, those who had carefully considered her questions went forward to the front of the church. My wife and I decided to join them. We realized that evening: to follow Christ requires a solemn, unwavering commitment.

God wants our help to bring in His harvest. Although He is understanding and compassionate, He's not interested in our excuses, only our sincerity and willingness.

**Dear Lord,** please forgive me for all the times I promised to follow You, but instead I charted my own path. If You still want me, I am Yours. In the holy name of Jesus, my Lord and Savior, I pray. Amen.

# In His Name

**He turned around and said to the spirit, "In the name of Jesus Christ I command you to come out of her!" At that moment the spirit left her** (Acts 16:18).

**Scripture:** Acts 16:16-24
**Song:** "We Rest on Thee"

The village elder, one who practiced sorcery, controlled the people of his African village by claiming to know the future. Among other things, he predicted the yield from future crops, the success of hunts, and the gender of unborn children.

Always nervous, the man twitched his head back and forth, never standing still, even for a moment. If a village member disagreed with him, he or she often became sick; some even died. Threatening retribution, he warned his villagers against accepting the newly appointed missionary. Anyone listening to Melvin's teachings about Jesus the Savior would surely perish.

When Melvin conducted church services, the village elder would attend, trying to disrupt them. Finally, Melvin told the spirit that controlled the man: "Be gone, in the name of Jesus!" The man ran off screaming, heading toward his nearby cave.

The next morning, the elder returned to the village square. He looked happy, no longer a bundle of nerves. He knelt down in front of the young missionary in the presence of the entire village and gave his life to Jesus. Other villagers followed. The name of Jesus Christ can save, heal, and deliver. Early Christians never hesitated to use it. And neither should we.

**Heavenly Father,** thanks for sending Your Son into this world and for giving us believers a name that is higher than any other name. Through Christ's name I pray. Amen.

# Some Are Listening

**Paul and Silas were praying and singing hymns to God, and the other prisoners were listening to them** (Acts 16:25).

**Scripture:** Acts 16:25-40
**Song:** "I Will Sing of the Mercies of the Lord"

Carl shuffled down Division Street in Portland, Oregon, his mind clouded, confused. He was looking to score again. He hated using drugs, but somehow, he could no longer say no. Maybe someone in the homeless camp, hidden on the nearby hillside, would help him out.

Carl turned left at the church property. The congregation was conducting its evening service. Mumbling to himself, "That's funny — the church should have dismissed by now — it's almost 10:30 p.m.," he decided to hang around to beg for some cash.

Meanwhile, the singing continued. "Why haven't they stopped yet?" Carl moved closer. "What's happening in there?" Now he could hear people praying inside. A divine compulsion slowly drew him through the front doors — and that's when he felt a warming presence. He dropped to the floor and wept for what seemed like hours. When Carl stood again, his life had changed; he would never abuse drugs again.

Most of the time, we don't consider prayer and worship as being witnessing tools, but they are. They can influence those who are listening in, and in some cases, might even inspire people to a brand new faith in God.

**Dear God,** I love praying and singing praises to Your name. It draws me close to You, and I can feel Your presence. If seekers can feel Your presence as well, then may I pray and worship everywhere I go! In Jesus' name, amen.

# Help Wanted

**A vision appeared to Paul in the night. A man of Macedonia stood and pleaded with him, saying, "Come over to Macedonia and help us"** (Acts 16:8, 9, *New King James Version*).

**Scripture:** Acts 16:1-5, 8-15
**Song:** "The Vision"

While in prayer one evening, Melvin heard the word *Africa* whispered in his ear. A few months later, he saw a vision of an outreached hand and heard the same voice saying, "Take my hand, and I will lead you to a place where you are needed." That's when Melvin began to seek divine guidance about going to Africa as a missionary.

He applied to the mission board of his church, and they assigned him to the Gold Coast, in Africa. However, before Melvin could begin his term, the missions department halted all outgoing missionaries due to financial concerns.

When the money crisis eased, they reassigned Melvin to India. His heart sank, because this change contradicted his call and vision. Nevertheless, he accepted the appointment and started raising funds. Just before his departure in 1955, the mission board switched his assignment again. They had an urgent need for someone in the Gold Coast.

God calls every Christian to minister somewhere. He may use a dream, a vision, an inward voice that speaks to our spirits — and sometimes, even a daily devotional reading.

**Dear God,** I realize the harvest is plentiful and the laborers are few. I am open to Your call and ready to serve as one of those laborers. Please show me where my help is needed the most. In Your name, I pray. Amen.

# The Greatness of Our God

**I will proclaim the name of the LORD. Oh, praise the greatness of our God!** (Deuteronomy 32:3).

**Scripture:** Deuteronomy 32:1-12
**Song:** "I Could Sing of Your Love Forever"

Hooked up to tubes and monitors, my grandson Luke lay motionless in his little bassinet in the Neonatal Intensive Care Unit (NICU). He was born without a diaphragm, and doctors gave him only a 30% chance of surviving. Parents and grandparents took turns holding his tiny hands and praying before and after surgery—a procedure to move his liver and intestines down into the abdominal area and install an artificial diaphragm.

Doctors and nurses worked around the clock. They relied on modern medicine and equipment. Some babies didn't go home from NICU, but I prayed as if Luke's life depended on my prayers.

When we brought our baby home from the hospital, I felt like Moses when he sang, "I will proclaim the name of the Lord. Oh, praise the greatness of our God!"

Moses experienced God's miracles through a 40-year journey in the wilderness. My family continues to witness the miracles of Luke's life, 10 years after his difficult birth. He is a constant reminder to us of how God drew us closer to himself and to each other.

Thank You, **Father God,** for never leaving me to suffer alone. It is wonderful to know You are with me in troubling times. I proclaim Your greatness, through Christ. Amen.

November 16–22. **Sue Tornai** lives with her husband, John, and dog, Maggie, in Carmichael, California. They enjoy vacationing at Lake Almanor in Northern California.

## Our God Is Near

**I have set my rainbow in the clouds, and it will be the sign of the covenant between me and the earth** (Genesis 9:13).

**Scripture:** Genesis 9:8-17
**Song:** "It Is Well with My Soul"

On March 11, 2011, Japan suffered a massive earthquake — of 9.0 magnitude — that triggered a 23-foot tsunami. The waves swept away homes, cars, boats, and trains, and caused the meltdown of two nuclear power plants. It took more than 16,000 lives and left nearly 6,000 people injured. Many who could return to their homes were afraid of contamination.

Scenes of the disaster made me wonder what it might have looked like when waters covered the earth in Noah's day. God promised that He would never again destroy the earth with water; He put His rainbow in the clouds to remind us of His vow.

People might have questioned whether God would keep His promises when the waves washed away so much property and life. The cost of damages (more than $300 billion) was the most in world history. But by the end of 2011, the spending involved in Japan's recovery increased its economy by 6.2%.

Even though it appeared as if the water might wash the country away, it didn't. God kept His Word. The rebuilding and restoration we have seen shows the resilience of people made in God's image. He doesn't abandon us human beings, but is with us through the storms and the reconstruction. He is as close as the cries of our hearts.

**Father**, You are worthy of praise, and I praise You. Thank You for being with me, even when I least expect it. Thank You for keeping Your promises. In Jesus' name, amen.

# Awesome God

**I will make you into a great nation, and I will bless you; I will make your name great, and you will be a blessing** (Genesis 12:2)

**Scripture:** Genesis 12:1-4
**Song:** "Our God Is an Awesome God"

No medicine or supplies arrived at Rwanguba Hospital for more than six weeks. Dr. Filipe could not give aid to the refugees who came from Rwanda. He thought he would have to close the doors. Against all odds he knelt and pleaded with God, "O Lord, I cannot look into the empty, longing eyes of people I am unable to help. Please send us a miracle."

Like Abram, Dr. Filipe trusted God . . . because he *had* to. Abram had no clue where he was going when he left Haran, but he believed God, and it was credited to him as righteousness. Dr. Filipe had no one else to turn to, so he turned to the one who had the answer.

A plane landed on an open field near the hospital the next day. The rugged-looking pilots jumped to the ground. "We found these boxes filled with medical supplies on our docks," one of the men said. "We didn't know what we were supposed to do with them, but we thought of you and the hospital."

Zana, the doctor's wife, smiled. "We serve an awesome God." Without delay, she and Dr. Filipe carried the boxes to the hospital and began giving the patients their treatments.

Thank You, **Precious Lord,** for the miracles of our faith. Thank You for the example of Abram, whom You honored as righteous. Help me to trust You as he did. In the name of Jesus, my Savior, I pray. Amen.

# His Inescapable Presence

**What is mankind that you are mindful of them, human beings that you care for them?** (Psalm 8:4).

**Scripture:** Psalm 8
**Song:** "How Majestic Is Your Name"

It was a Saturday night, and I drove to a nearby bakery, thinking a piece of French silk pie would ease the pain of my loneliness. When the perky waitress said, "We're fresh out," I couldn't keep the tears from rolling down my cheeks. "I'm sorry," she said. "We have other delicious choices."

Embarrassed, I later realized I'd tried to meet a spiritual need with a physical solution. Back at my apartment, I cried out to God, "I don't want to go on anymore!"

It was as if the Father met me at the point of my deepest need, wrapped His arms around me and whispered, "Could you make it another day if I stay with you?"

I felt His amazing love surround me. "I guess so," I whispered. I dusted off my Bible and began to read. Every word seemed to speak directly to me and melt my heart.

Soon I was reading the Bible and praying every morning before I went to work. Sometimes I didn't know what to pray. All I could say was, "Thank You, Jesus. Thank You, Jesus for loving me."

Many times I've wondered to myself, *Who am I that the God of creation would care for me?* I am glad He does.

Thank You, **Father God,** for surprising me with Your amazing love. Thank You for loving me when I didn't love myself. It means so much to know You are always with me. In the precious name of Jesus my Lord. Amen.

# Blessing in Disguise

**We wait in hope for the LORD; he is our help and our shield** (Psalm 33:20).

**Scripture:** Psalm 33:13-22
**Song:** "Count Your Blessings"

My friend Carol suffered through the last days of her husband's ill health and subsequent death, and she often left the hospital in tears. But one afternoon she did something she normally wouldn't do. She drove through an intersection on a yellow light. That is not what the citation read. It said the light was *red* and it included a picture, a $750 fine, and a court date.

Carol held the ticket in her hand a few days after her husband's funeral, tears streamed down her face. Where would the money come from? She bowed her head and prayed Psalm 33:20, with first-person pronouns, "I wait in hope for the Lord; He is my help and my shield."

Carol trusted God through those dark hours. Since she had never been in trouble, the courtroom frightened her. God provided a police officer to speak for her before the judge, someone she refers to as "the angel in blue" to this day. In light of all Carol had been through with the loss of her husband, the judge forgave her the fine . . . if she would do community service.

Carol agreed and served in a nearby church. The work gave Carol the break she needed from her grieving. "That ticket must have been sent from Heaven," she says.

Thank You, **Lord**, for Your faithfulness, counsel, and powerful presence. I couldn't make it without Your love surrounding me and holding me as I walk through difficult days. In the name of the Father and of the Son and of the Holy Spirit, I pray. Amen.

# Praising God

**Clap your hands, all you nations; shout to God with cries of joy** (Psalm 47:1)

**Scripture:** Psalm 47
**Song:** "Everybody Clap Your Hands"

I had to tell Mama, who lay in a hospital bed with a terminal illness, that my 3-year-old grandson was rushed to the hospital for emergency surgery. "I wish I could hold him," she said. "I wish I could do something, but I can't even help myself."

"Luke needs your prayers," I said.

"I *can* pray," Mama replied. Lying in her hospital bed, trapped in her helplessness, she prayed, "Lord, who else can we turn to? You are the Great Physician, and we put our hope in you alone."

During the weeks that followed Luke's surgery, I prayed with Mama on the phone. When the doctor finally said we could bring him home, I couldn't wait to tell her. I heard her shout, "Praise God! Hallelujah!"

The next morning the nurses found Mama sitting up in bed, with her legs hanging off to the side—something she hadn't done for a long time. "What are you doing?" asked the nurse.

"I just want to dangle my feet," Mama said. No more earthly cares. No more pain and suffering. It was as if Mama was home, splashing her feet in a heavenly river. Then she lay back on her pillow. In that moment God did carry her home to be with Him forever.

**Praise God!** Hallelujah! You are a great and awesome God. Thank You for Your presence. Thank You for always being with me, especially during challenging times in my faith. Through Christ, amen.

# Life in Christ

**"In him we live and move and have our being."** As some of your own poets have said, **"We are his offspring"** (Acts 17:28).

**Scripture:** Acts 17:1-4, 10-12, 22-25, 28
**Song:** "In Christ Alone"

Dennis rode his bike into the country with only a sandwich and a Bible in his backpack. On a patch of grass under an old oak tree, he spent the day crying out to God because he didn't like his hippie lifestyle anymore. Yet, he had no clue what to do next. The words "follow the manufacturer's instructions" popped into his head, and he wondered why he heard those particular words.

Since he didn't know where to start reading, he opened the Bible to the center. His eyes fell on the words of Psalm 25:4. "Show me your ways, Lord, teach me your paths." That's what he wanted—to give up his crazy parties and live for the God of his youth.

When he went home, he told his wife the decision he'd made, and together they knelt in their living room and prayed a prayer of repentance and surrender to God.

Dennis says that he would not be living for Christ if his neighbors hadn't first showed him what that looked like. They had never judged him for the way he lived, but they'd certainly prayed for him regularly. And they had invited him to their church, where he found God's love at work in His people.

Thank You, **Lord God Almighty,** for not giving up on me. Thank You for second, third, and fourth chances. I invite You to live and move and have Your being in my life. I pray this prayer in the name of Jesus, my merciful Savior and Lord. Amen.

# Teachable?

**He guides the humble in what is right and teaches them his way** (Psalm 25:9).

**Scripture:** Psalm 25:8-12, 20, 21
**Song:** "O Master, Let Me Walk with Thee"

Nursing instructors sometimes prefer students who are a little apprehensive and who have no experience, as they begin the practical portion of their education in a hospital setting. Now working with real people in a dynamic setting, the eager students use their "book learning" as the foundation for "hands on" application. When they lack any previous experience, they're usually more *teachable*. Those with some background experience may not be as receptive to on-site instruction.

Jackie, a nursing instructor, told one of her students that she should take a particular newborn's temperature by placing the thermometer under the patient's armpit. One of her new students challenged Jackie. "When I worked as an aide in another hospital, the nurses always did this differently."

But Jackie clearly explained her reasons in the case of the infant before them. And, though obviously skeptical, the student nurse did what she was told to do.

Throughout His ministry years, our Lord encountered experts in religion who refused to be teachable. Yet any human being can only grow spiritually through an attitude of humility.

**Lord**, give me an attitude of humble expectancy each time I open Your Word. I want to grow in Christlikeness, ready to listen and to obey. In Jesus' name, amen.

November 23–29. Married for over 35 years, **Katherine Douglas** and her husband like to try something new each year. This year it's growing heirloom vegetables in their small garden.

# Waiting Without Whining

**Wait for the LORD; be strong and take heart and wait for the LORD** (Psalm 27:14).

**Scripture:** Psalm 27:4, 5, 8, 9, 11-14
**Song:** "Everlasting God"

Do you ever mumble or talk out loud when you're alone in the car? I do. It usually goes something like this: "Come on! The traffic light isn't getting any greener, my friend . . . Are you blind? Hey, get going!"

Of course, the person in the car ahead of me isn't my friend, because I don't know her. And we both know the traffic lights have three colors and not several hues. Fortunately, she can't hear my impatient "reminders." I work hard at keeping my hand off the horn (admittedly, not always successfully).

Waiting on, or for, something or someone often translates into more than inconvenience. So many times we must await medical test results or wait to hear news of friends ministering in dangerous places. Clearly, the Lord gives me—gives us all—ample opportunity to develop the virtue of patience.

The Lord tells us through David that we're not only to wait *on* the Lord, but we're to wait *for* Him too. "Be still before the LORD and wait patiently for him" (Psalm 37:7). Paul tells me as Christians we're "waiting for the coming of our Lord Jesus Christ" (1 Corinthians 1:7, *KJV*).

Whether I'm waiting *for* others or *on* them, I want to do it as unto the Lord, with calm kindness. No whining or fretting.

**Lord**, help me wait patiently on others as well as You. I pray to make the best use of waiting times and waiting rooms, as You work patience in me. Through Christ, amen.

# Woman with the Answers

**The wise in heart are called discerning, and gracious words promote instruction** (Proverbs 16:21).

**Scripture:** Proverbs 16:19-24
**Song:** "How Great the Wisdom"

Kristin, who once taught in elementary school classrooms, now zeroes in on helping children who struggle with reading. As a public school reading specialist, she has learned what books are particularly effective in creating a love of reading. She begins with books that kids want to read again and again.

One of those books for preschool children is titled *Don't Let the Pigeon Drive the Bus!* by Mo Willems. Kristin gave it as a gift (along with some other books) to our grandsons when she met them for the first time. My daughter, who plans on home schooling her sons, questioned Kristin on several topics related to schooling and learning. After Kristin left, our daughter was still marveling at my friend's wealth of knowledge and insight. "She's like the answer woman, isn't she?"

The truths of Proverbs continue today. Have you ever had a speaker regale you with his funny stories or delight you with an object lesson? If you're like me, you may often remember the object lesson or the funny stories, but . . . not the point made!

Words spoken graciously and with straightforward wisdom—like those of my friend—stay with us long after theatrics and object lessons have faded from our minds.

**God of grace and glory,** thanks for the wise counsel of friends. And I praise You too, for those You bring into my life who help me to be more discerning. Give me Your wisdom this day and always. Through Christ I pray. Amen.

# Water and the Word

**Therefore go and make disciples of all nations** (Matthew 28:19).

**Scripture:** Matthew 28:16-20
**Song:** "Holy, Holy, Holy, Lord, Thy Disciples"

For years Doug and Karen have worked among the poor in the arid country of Burkina Faso in west Africa. In addition to sharing the gospel message, this couple has also been involved in digging village wells. Once this basic need is met, they often find listeners willing to receive the story of Christ, the one who offers living water (see John 4:10).

During a recent trip to check out a site for a well in a poor village, this missionary couple was unable to stay and do any teaching. With heartache they wrote in an e-mail, "The village chief was disappointed. He wanted us to stay right then and tell his people about Jesus." Though water was needed, this chief had a greater burden for the spiritual thirst of his people.

I aspire to be like that man. I want to share the gospel with my friends and neighbors. Physical needs are many and can over-whelm us all, but may I keep in view the greatest need of all: that people hear the glorious, saving message of forgiveness of sins in the cross of Christ. Since "All authority in heaven and earth has been given" to Christ (v. 18), I know I don't have to be a foreign missionary to participate in making disciples. I can do that important work right where I am.

Use me, **Lord,** not only as a disciple, but as a disciple maker. I pray for the leading of your Holy Spirit in doing my part in mentoring others. I pray this in the name of Him who has all authority, the Lord Jesus Christ. Amen.

# How Do You Spell That?

**I know you by name and you have found favor with me** (Exodus 33:12).

**Scripture:** Exodus 33:12-17
**Song:** "He Knows My Name"

Ted came across a former acquaintance on the street. The man greeted him by name and began asking him about his family and other mutual friends. As Ted stood there answering his questions and asking some of his own, he knew he was stymied. *He simply could not remember the man's name!*

Is this a member from one of my previous churches? Do I know him from the gym? From my high school days? Lord, please don't let him be one of my wife's bazillion relatives!

Ted decided to ease his way out of the situation with a trick he learned as a minister. Before they went their separate ways, he asked, "How do you spell your last name again?"

The man's face contorted slightly. "S-m-i-t-h."

Ted has not used that little "trick" again.

Our great God never has to ask our names. And, thankfully, Jesus tells us that our Father knows far more than our names. He knows us so well that the hairs on our head aren't just counted for a grand total. God has actually *numbered* each one (see Matthew 10:30). Whenever we feel as if we're "just a number," or a faceless person in the crowd, we can know that the one who created us remembers our names—and a whole lot more.

Thank You, **Father,** that I'm Your child and that You know me by name. Thank You for the assurances from Your Word that I'm valuable to You. In the name of Him whose name is Wonderful, amen.

# Elder Care—for the Younger Ones

**They invited him to their home and explained to him the way of God more adequately** (Acts 18:26).

**Scripture:** Acts 18:24-28
**Song:** "Tell Me the Story of Jesus"

When we hear the phrase "elder care," most of us think about caring for the aged. Yet there may be another kind of elder care that benefits younger generations more than the older generation.

Betty used to host backyard barbecues in the summer months, and she served up cocoa and cookies in the wintertime. She invited young teens, most of whom had just come to trust in Christ for salvation, to her home for food and fun. Yet her primary purpose was to expose these young people to the application of the Word of God to every area of their lives.

Dick did a similar thing. He led Bible studies in the homes of young couples so they might get established in the Word. He encouraged his students to study the Bible so they wouldn't be duped by religious charlatans or messages of "name it and claim it" for material prosperity. Dick, like Betty, was an elder in the faith and cared deeply about helping new Christians grow in the faith of the Lord Jesus.

Some of us may be called upon to provide elder care for an aging parent. Yet opportunities surround us now for encouraging and mentoring those younger in the faith than we are. As the elders, we must care for them.

**Father,** I want to be an encourager. Use me to lovingly and kindly mentor those younger in the faith, especially those in my own family. In Jesus' name, amen.

# Dive In!

**Paul lived and worked with them, for they were tentmakers just as he was** (Acts 18:3, *New Living Translation*).

**Scripture:** Acts 18:1-11, 18-21
**Song:** "Your Mission"

Anna and her husband, Mike, recently relocated to another country as international workers. Planning to work in their outreach center in the heart of a coastal city, they thought everything was in place for them. But then the government began making changes in the rules for expatriates.

If the couple wanted to remain, they'd have to contribute more to the local economy in other lines of work. Anna was granted permission to help in women's ministries at the center, but Mike must work elsewhere—and he found just the thing: training nationals in scuba diving and snorkeling.

As an experienced scuba instructor, Mike could start this new venture. And by establishing a new business, he'd help the local economy while gaining new opportunities in ministry and outreach.

Centuries ago, Paul the apostle used his secular training to help supplement his income and to avoid stressing his struggling young churches any further. Today missionaries are doing it throughout the world. My part is to prayerfully encourage and monetarily support, those on the front lines of gospel proclamation.

**Father,** I pray for those who minister throughout the world—many of them in dangerous places—as they preach the good news of salvation in Jesus. Give them courage and wisdom as they often work in hostile cultures. Through Christ, amen.

# Out of Nothing at All?

**[God] rested from all the work of creating that he had
done** (Genesis 2:3).

**Scripture:** Genesis 1:28–2:3
**Song:** "Creator of the Earth and Sky"

Christians have always affirmed that what God did "in the
beginning" (v. 1) was *ex nihilo*, "out of nothing." There is a clear
distinction between making and creating something. To *make* is
to gather existing materials and form something different. But
to *create* is to bring about something more than just different.
What comes to be, from God, is what has never been before.

Do you believe only God can accomplish such a feat? Or could
it be that humans will be able to pull off an *ex nihilo* exploit?

God was once approached by a scientist who says, "God, we've
decided we don't need You anymore. These days we can clone
people, transplant organs, and do all sorts of miraculous things."

And God says: "Suppose we have a man-making contest'"?

"You're on!" replies the scientist.

"Well, now," says the Lord. "We'll do it the way I did it with
the first man, Adam, OK?"

"Fine" agrees the scientist as he bends down to scoop up a
handful of dirt.

"Whoa!" says God. "Not so fast. You get your own dirt."

**Lord God of Creation**, I am so thankful that You are omnipotent and sovereign, not
only in the universe but in my life. Keep me walking according to Your will and rejoicing in Your power to guard my soul until the last day. Through Christ, amen.

Nov. 30. **Gary Wilde** is a minister living in Venice, Florida, with his wife, Carol. His twin boys were
both recently married.

# My Prayer Notes